Cambridge Elements

Elements in Defence Economics
edited by
Keith Hartley
University of York

DEFENCE ECONOMICS AND INNOVATION

Gustavo Fornari Dall'Agnol
Federal University of Santa Catarina

CAMBRIDGE
UNIVERSITY PRESS

Shaftesbury Road, Cambridge CB2 8EA, United Kingdom

One Liberty Plaza, 20th Floor, New York, NY 10006, USA

477 Williamstown Road, Port Melbourne, VIC 3207, Australia

314–321, 3rd Floor, Plot 3, Splendor Forum, Jasola District Centre,
New Delhi – 110025, India

103 Penang Road, #05–06/07, Visioncrest Commercial, Singapore 238467

Cambridge University Press is part of Cambridge University Press & Assessment,
a department of the University of Cambridge.

We share the University's mission to contribute to society through the pursuit of
education, learning and research at the highest international levels of excellence.

www.cambridge.org
Information on this title: www.cambridge.org/9781009517348

DOI: 10.1017/9781009409766

When citing this work, please include a reference to the DOI 10.1017/9781009409766

First published 2024

A catalogue record for this publication is available from the British Library

ISBN 978-1-009-51734-8 Hardback
ISBN 978-1-009-40974-2 Paperback
ISSN 2632-332X (online)
ISSN 2632-3311 (print)

Cambridge University Press & Assessment has no responsibility for the persistence
or accuracy of URLs for external or third-party internet websites referred to in this
publication and does not guarantee that any content on such websites is, or will
remain, accurate or appropriate.

Defence Economics and Innovation

Elements in Defence Economics

DOI: 10.1017/9781009409766
First published online: December 2024

Gustavo Fornari Dall'Agnol
Federal University of Santa Catarina

Author for correspondence: Gustavo Fornari Dall'Agnol, gustfd@gmail.com

Abstract: This Element presents an analytical model for assessing the success or failure of innovative large-scale defence projects. To achieve this goal, it constructs a theoretical model based on a three-angle analysis: the International System, the innovative potential, and the domestic political arena. Each angle of analysis generates an independent variable, namely: level of threat, technological feasibility, and political consensus. It is held that technological feasibility and political consensus are necessary and conjointly sufficient conditions to explain the success or failure of large-scale defence projects. The success of the innovative defence projects is strongly and positively related to the level of external threat. The initial hypothesis is tested by scrutinizing three specific projects in the United States (Future Combat Systems (FCS), The B-2 Stealth Bomber and the F-35). The conclusion is that the model is sound and might be generalized to analyse the prospects of success or failure of other large-scale defence projects.

Keywords: defence policy, innovation, economics, decision-making, project management

ISBNs: 9781009517348 (HB), 9781009409742 (PB), 9781009409766 (OC)
ISSNs: 2632-332X (online), 2632-3311 (print)

Contents

1 Introduction

In this Element, I aim to explain the success or failure of large-scale defence projects. The guiding question is: why do long-term large-scale defence projects succeed or fail? This question logically entails other issues: what are the main causal factors that impact the outcome of the project? How and by whom are the key decisions made? In order provide an explanation, I will first propose a theoretical framework based on a linear model of causality with three independent variables determining the variation in the level of success or failure. The success criteria (SC) are drawn from project management literature adapted to defence and its strategic industry idiosyncrasies. Each independent variable derives from a different angle of analysis: (i) the level of innovative potential, (ii) the International System, and (iii) the domestic political arena. The main thesis of this Element can be stated as follows: innovative potential is translated into a sine qua non variable, in this case, technological feasibility, which is the ability to accomplish the project's technical and operational goals. The threat level is considered to be positively and strongly related to the success of a large-scale project, but it is not a *necessary* condition. In relation to the domestic political arena, it is argued that the level of success of a project depends on a minimum level of consensus, or at least, broad agreement among and within the Executive and Congress and its key stakeholders and it is also a necessary condition for the success of a project. Each of these variables and their relation to the dependent variable – level of success and failure of large-scale projects – is presented in more detail next. The projects are assessed through three angles of analysis.

Considering the *dependent* variable, the literature has evolved in evaluating the success or failure of projects. Whereas previously the focus was on efficiency, which encompasses time, costs, and performance, more recently a large set of variables (success factors) have been tested and related to success criteria. To establish proper success criteria, some premises are mandatory, for example optimization of resources. Therefore, the three parameters of efficiency outlined earlier in this section are part of the proposed variation of success. Decision-maker needs, operational capacity, and proved successful engagement are the complementary SC applied here and denominated 'effectiveness criteria'. I argue that in defence, efficiency is subordinated to effectiveness. I focus on large-scale defence projects fitting Department of Defense's (DoD) category of Major Acquisition Programs, as defined in US Code § 2430 and is expected to exceed $1.8 billion in 1990 dollars (LII, 2022). A further focus is on innovative military projects, defined by Steven Rosen as 'a change in the concepts of operation of that combat arm, which is the ideas governing the ways it uses its forces to win a campaign' (Rosen, 1991, p. 7). I have chosen a failed project, a project on the failed spectrum and a project on the successful spectrum (FCS; B-2; F-35) in accordance with the methodology proposed: to isolate the causal links that are present or absent in the same phenomena.

There is no objective way of evaluating success or failure in absolute terms. Nonetheless, if a program is cancelled without meeting any criteria of success, it will be considered a failed project. If a project is completed satisfying all criteria, it will be considered successful. Projects in between will be classified on the 'failure spectrum' if they do not meet minimum success criteria, and on the 'success spectrum' if they meet most success criteria. This research starts from the premise that effectiveness is more important than efficiency because defence development requirements are considered subordinate to economic calculations in the face of urgent military needs. The concept and parameters outlined in this section are indispensable to achieve the goals of this Element. A project can suffer significant delays and cost overruns and still be considered on the successful spectrum.

Thus, the success criteria to be used here are the following:

- Cost overruns (initial estimate compared to final cost in %)
- Schedule overruns (initial estimate compared to cancellation/deployment)
- Performance: meeting design goals (tests, deployment)
- Stakeholder's need (government)
- Operational success (satisfaction with operations utilizing the innovation).

I will now present briefly the three independent variables, which will be fully examined in the subsequent part of the Element. The first independent variable (X1) is technological feasibility. Innovation is systemic, evolutionary, and synergistic, and depends on a complementary and reinforcing relation among the main actors involved. It needs, in the first place, a solid mobilization of resources and personnel. The study of highly innovative projects imposes a challenge since innovation is, by nature, extremely risky. It is impossible to know ex ante whether the project will work. If it works and the project enters acquisition, the analysis may become tautological. However, this Element proposes analysing technological feasibility through the lifecycle of a project. The elasticity of demand over the duration of the project provides solid evidence of the impacts of technical feasibility on decision-making. Assessment from different *senior players* and specialists also helps to establish the project's technological feasibility.

The second variable (X2) is threat level. No precise measure of threat level exists, although it is possible to demonstrate a clear relation to innovation. In order to do so, threat level is divided into the ways it affects large-scale defence projects. The first is situated on a *longue durée* spectrum and relies on ontological premises derived from a realist perspective. In this Element, I explore this matter reviewing neorealist and historical sociology/Second-Image Reversed perspectives.[1] According to this perspective, one can argue that defence budgets fluctuate in the long-term in correlation with the imperatives of the International System. However, this research is focused on specific large-scale projects, be they situated in long-term innovative cycles or not. The second aspect is that threat level, accessed through the relative distribution of power and measured in a proxy manner (Data base: Correlates of War (COW)), triggers innovation. From this viewpoint, there is, in the linear model, an ontological precedence of threat in relation to X1 and X2. The third, and equally complicated, variation on threat level is direct threat. This can be measured by identifying incidents between the main adversaries through the lifecycle of the project. In this case, geographical factors, Clausewitzian friction, and perception must rely on a *ceteris paribus* condition.

The third independent variable (X3) is political consensus. A minimum level of consensus is a necessary condition for the success of large-scale projects. Many authors and theories put forward the main domestic variables that define decision-making and defence. In this Element, *three premises* are drawn from engagement in theoretical debate: (i) leaders tend to make suboptimal decisions (Simon's Bounded Rationality); (ii) the results of a decision are determined by the potential consensus built from the pulling and hauling of senior players; (iii) senior players, including the main bureaucracies, regardless of ideological ideology or intended goodwill in intentions, act, in as, protecting self-interests by maximizing budget, prestige, and area of operation. Congress and the Executive are the two pillars of defence and foreign policy decision-making, and the budgetary process and legislation is the central arena where the pulling and hauling takes place. Broad consensus will have a positive correlation with the success of innovation. In a pulling and hauling scenario which characterizes US domestic politics, implementing policy, especially considering the use of a large part of the budget, must count on building a coalition or consensus among and within Congress and the Executive, with a special emphasis on senior players and key bureaucracies (e.g., General Accounting Office; Congressional Budget Committee; Armed Forces) which can substantially affect the results agreed between Congress and the Executive.

An initial and provisional model may be presented as in Figure 1.

---

[1] Neorealism is a theory of International Relations which holds that the systemic structure of the system constrains the actions of the units (states), compelling them towards a *self-help* situation for survival in a competitive structure. As for Second Image-Reversed, it explores the external forces which have causal effects in domestic development.

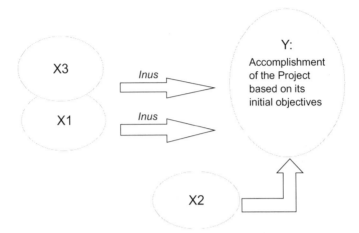

Figure 1 Venn diagram (construction of the model)

Source: Dall'Agnol, 2022, p. 27. The author.

Taking into consideration the premises and conceptual framework of the variables presented, I argue that X1 and X3 are necessary and conjointly sufficient to explain to success or failure of large-scale projects. X2 is strongly and positively related to the success of such innovations. The use of linear logic is a promising starting point, but it needs a complementary methodological step. A provisional systemic model which encompasses the relations among the variables is, thus, presented in the next section. For the purpose of analysis, however, I will also evaluate each variable in isolation. *Inus* conditions stands for an insufficient, but necessary part of an unnecessary but sufficient condition.

The main idea of this Element is to relate the proposed premises and resulting causal model to the SC of large-scale defence projects. Each of the three independent variables has three parameters, which will score from *low* to *high*. Technological feasibility is assessed through observing demand elasticity together with stakeholder's positions and assessment of the project by experts throughout its lifecycle. Political consensus is evaluated by analysing decisions and positions of senior players within Congress and the Executive. Finally, external threat is evaluated mainly by the relative distribution of capabilities among states. For each variable, a score (low, medium or high) is assigned in order to evaluate their impact and draw conclusions regarding their causal weight on the level of success of large-scale defence projects.

Some limitations of the model must be outlined. It is specific to the US decision-making structure and if it were to expand to projects in other countries, it would have to be adapted. This is true especially in countries where decision-making is extremely centralized. Furthermore, as a great power, external threat for the United States is different from states like Bolivia, for example, which are not engaged in great power competition and whose threats come mainly from other causes, such as regional security dynamics. Lastly, countries which lack the resources and ability to innovate would have to be treated in other terms, with import and export considerations given more weight in the analysis. The United States is also involved in international projects and is a major exporter of military equipment. The model here does not investigate such projects.

1.1 Three Angles of Analysis

I have outlined the conditions which affect the success or failure of large-scale defence projects, taking into consideration the initial goals of such projects and the SC established in the Introduction section. I proposed a provisional model defining the necessary and sufficient conditions for the success of such projects. I now present a provisional enhanced model based on the discussion about the relation among the independent variables. The model encompasses a *systemic* relation between the three angles of analysis proposed here. The logic of the theoretical framework is systemic, albeit it is closely related to a linear causal model.

There are strong interconnections among the independent variables. For instance, there is a *systemic* relation between X1 and X3: as the project advances, technological feasibility doubts are mitigated, although the more difficult and costly the proposed innovation, the more likely the project will fail to gain support. In an urgent scenario, the tendency is that stakeholder's needs prevail and cost issues and opposing arguments weaken. Stakeholder needs may involve perception, although this aspect is beyond the scope of this Element – and is addressed *en passant* only. To recognize the interconnections, an *enhanced* model needs to be constructed.

The refinement of a linear causal model entails regarding the first model in a *systemic* way in the sense that the variables interact and reinforce one another. Technological feasibility considerations affect the senior players' view of and support for the project, and consequently the resources devoted to it. Pulling and hauling among different actors affects technological feasibility since the resources fluctuate and affect the choice to spend on the project as opposed to other perceived priorities and projects with a stronger political support. The external environment influences both technological feasibility and political support, since mobilizing resources and personnel strongly correlates with direct threat and distribution of power. Long-term investment is also affected by general threat level. In a scenario with large long-term competition, defence

Defence Economics

spending increases, and decision-makers devote their attention to large-scale projects, making continuous effort on R&D and innovation mandatory. In this level of abstraction, even if the specific project fails, spinoffs, spin-ins, and the impacts of military spending are taken into consideration. Nonetheless, the Element does not focus on this last correlation, given the focus on specific projects. If innovation is successful, threat tends to diminish.

The three independent variables – external threat, domestic political consensus, and technological/innovative potential – are indeed broad. However, the choice was not made solely by considering the benefits of parsimony. These variables can be operationalized in empirical studies and the theory can be broadened by utilizing jointly the qualitative and quantitative parameters. The premises held here are sufficient to explain the success or failure or large-scale defence projects. If one tried to incorporate all domestic variables which may impact defence decision-making, the study would be reduced to analysis and not theory. Regarding decision-making, the theoretical framework encompasses other possible variables in the positions of senior players. Managerial or engineering problems regarding specific projects are also reflected in the *proxy* parameters chosen to access the viability of innovation. As for external threat, I argue that accompanied by *en passant* idiosyncrasies, the materialistic perspective held here is best to explain the impacts of the external environment on specific projects.

Taking into consideration the results of this part, the systemic model can be visualized as given in Figure 2.

Figure 2 is an illustration of the systemic character of innovation and the parameters for success and failure of defence projects, to be further developed in this Element. Section 2 deepens the analysis of the three independent variables: literature review, premises, and parameters for comparison and correlation. Three main topics are divided by the angles of analysis: technological feasibility (TF),

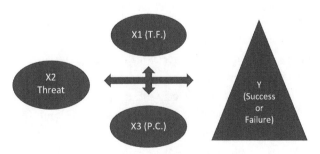

Figure 2 The systemic model of large-scale defence project's success or failure
Source: The Author.

external threat, and political consensus (PC). The project must be feasible – although, if addressed ex ante, it is impossible to determine its feasibility. Ex post would make the analysis tautological. So, in relation to the other variables, during the lifecycle of the project, technological feasibility can be estimated. A project needs a minimum level of consensus among senior players such as Congressional Acquisition Committees and the Executive to go further in the acquisition and budgetary arena. This relates to stakeholder's need and stands on the progress of the project. Back to external threat (X2) it has a causal strong relationship with both the development of technology and with forming a political consensus. No decision-maker will risk engaging major threats without mobilizing a large number of resources and personnel. That includes R&D to assure technological feasibility.

The Element is organized as it follows. Section 2.1 deals with innovation and defence economics, outlining main concepts such as Defence Industrial Base (DIB), procurement, military spending, and technological feasibility. Section 2.2 engages – objectively and briefly – with different theoretical perspectives which investigate the impacts of the International System on state behaviour, such as neorealism, internal balancing, second image reversed, and historical sociology. Section 2.3 addresses the debates around bureaucratic theory and other theories of decision-making: Advocacy Coalition Framework; punctuated-equilibrium; veto-player, neoclassical realism, elite, and pluralist theories. The main hypothesis and auxiliary hypotheses are detailed at the end of the section. For the purpose of building a *model*, only the main arguments are put forward. In short, the main thesis of this Element is that threat level is strongly and positively related to the success or failure of innovative large-scale projects and technological feasibility and political consensus are necessary and conjointly sufficient conditions to explain it.

Section 3 applies the theoretical framework and general model to comparative case studies. I propose here the main facts that relate to the parameters and indexes generated from the model. The case studies are the future combat systems, the B-2 bomber, and the F-35. The conclusion summarizes the main findings presenting a table to measure the success or failure of large-scale projects, and it draws attention to the limitations of the research as well as proposing future research possibilities.

The methodology I propose is based on the Historical Comparative Method. The comparative method aims at establishing empirical causal relations between two or more variables, while others are kept constant. In this way, it utilizes a *ceteris paribus* condition (Lijphart, 1971). Usually, the comparative method engages in a limited number of cases (*small-n*), that is, it is recommended as an intermediate strategy between case studies and *large-n* quantitative studies. The present research, through theoretical dialogue, can also be placed on the *theory-confirming, theory infirming, and theory building* spectrum, depending on the result of the comparative case analysis. Epistemologically, it is situated between nomothetical and idiographic approaches. It has the advantage of identifying the factors present or not in the same phenomena, thus allowing the inference of causal links. Theory building and testing are the purpose of this Element. The method is mainly qualitative, although the parameters outlined advance the use of quantitative techniques.

Finally, a brief remark on data. The data for external threat is inevitably drawn partially from arbitrary analysis. However, COW database will work as a proxy, alongside conceptual definitions, to obtain the proposed assessment of success or failure. The index is composed of the distribution of key material capabilities among states. As for political consensus, Senate Armed Service Committee, House Armed Service Committee, and floor opposition in terms of budget decisions and voting are used alongside Congressional Budget Office (CBO) and other specialist evaluations. The military services, special-ized bureaus stands (such as the General Accountability Office (GAO)), and the civil Executive authorities' official positions and decisions are used for com-parison among cases. Projected costs and real acquisition figures are assessed in order to complement the analysis.

2 Defence and Innovation

Although the theme of this study is better suited to the discipline of Defence Economics, the inclusion of variables addressed at both the theoretical and empirical levels include the pursuit of power and wealth. In this sense, it might be more appropriately termed Political Economy of Defence. Hence, Sections 2.2 and 2.3 are dedicated to international politics and the disputes of the domestic political arena. This choice is based on the need to avoid the risk of omitting important variables, which impact the outcomes of large-scale defence projects. Section 2.1, however, builds the main basis of the theoretical frame-work and it aims at delineating the central concepts and themes of Defence Economics and how they are related to large-scale defence projects. Since this is the ground for my theoretical and empirical contribution, I hold that it is a theme that belongs essentially to the discipline of Defence Economics as defined by Keith Hartley (2020) in this series, tackling issues of the distribution of scarce resources in defence.

Social phenomena are complex and thus involve a wide range of possible causality mechanisms. As I argue, some level of arbitrariness, even in complex multivariate regressions or neural networks, is unavoidable. Nevertheless, a student of such phenomena can infer the most important variables by deduction and observation. These phenomena, including the one investigated here, are embedded in an economic and *systemic* structure. Some actors have more weight than others and must work through different channels – which translate into processes – for specific issues. Consequently, the next three sections aim at situating large-scale defence projects in this framework of analysis, generating a hypothesis and a systematic relation among them, as proposed in the Introduction section. Evidence is provided in Section 2.1. However, the theoretical framework proposed is only briefly outlined.

2.1 Defence Economics and Large-Scale Projects

Defence economics is a relatively new field. Important advances have been made by pioneer authors such as Peck and Scherer (1962) in analysing the acquisition process, and Olsen and Zeckhouser (1966) engaging with military alliances.[2] More recently, many authors have contributed to the field in diverse areas such as (i) efficiency models, (ii) procurement and acquisition, (iii) geopolitical aid, and (iv) budget, to cite a few. Distribution of resources is important for society's general well-being. The well-known *guns versus butter* dilemma puts in question how much should be spent on building military capabilities and, as a consequence, investing in large-scale projects. Moreover, if a project succeeds, it might generate a security *output* to the country in question and produce possible *spillovers* (e.g., semiconductors, GPS, internet, jet powered turbines, and so on). On the other hand, if it fails, sunken costs are its most immediate but not the only result, although not the only ones. Scarce resources could have been used otherwise, for example, on health, education, and even other military priorities. Studies demonstrate that civil towards military *spin-ins* have surpassed *spin-offs*. A distinctive feature of defence markets is their monopsonic character. The role of the government and decision-making has effects on both the supply side and the demand side. A government can, for example, cancel a project. This makes entry barriers higher since firms have to have *expertise* in military tactics as well as government procurement policy. As opposed to regular markets, defence outputs are hard to measure. Besides the cited *spillovers*, objective ways of finding an output are difficult. Defence is thus seen as a public good, providing security for the country. However, there is no precise measure of defence outputs. It is generally seen as a public good, providing security and peace. In alliances, for example, they fit public good criteria being non-excludable and non-rival outputs.

In this section, I attempt to construct the conceptual basis to assess a large-scale project in defence economics. I start by proposing one of the main variables,

---

[2] A critique of Olsen and Zeckhauser's analysis can be found in Dall'Agnol and Dall'Agnol, 2020.

namely technological feasibility. This variable is difficult to operationalize and must rely on *proxy* parameters and a historical account of the project and variations throughout its lifecycle. Before presenting the main concepts, it is necessary to state that innovation is understood differently in economics than in military preparedness. Here I focus on the economic analysis and the variety of economic issues which affect large-scale projects.

2.1.1 Innovation

The projects I analyse in this Element are highly innovative. They belong to what may be considered a strategic industry. These endeavours are at the forefront of the technological frontier: they are highly technological and R&D-intensive industries with technical spillovers. They are decreasing-cost industries reflecting scale and learning economies. In the defence sector, innovations are demanded by governments, and few industries compete to meet their requirements. In the field of economics, business practices, logistics, marketing methods, and institutional rearrangement are considered innovation. Here, I focus on product innovation.

Innovation is, by definition, risky. Furthermore, as briefly outlined, they are systemic and evolutionary, depending on a variety of factors and idiosyncrasies that affect their outcome. Firms that undertake the risk of innovation, especially in defence, are susceptible to the risk of losing important long-term contracts. I demonstrate that only a few firms provide weapon systems to the United States, since relying only on government contracts exacerbates the risk and the industry must count on solid incentives, usually provided by the government in the form of R&D funding and follow-on contracts. Northrop Grumman, having had the B-2 stealth bomber program cancelled during George H. W Bush's presidency, suffered a major setback. While innovating, firms expect the benefits of extraordinary profits for their radical innovations. Appropriability is a particularly important concept when addressing innovation. It refers to the power incentives, in terms of extraordinary profits, to undertaking the risk of innovation (Schumpeter, 1934, 1966).

Furthermore, the enforcement of intellectual property rights is especially sensitive in the defence sector, dampening the benefits of innovating. Secrecy, lead time, non-disclosure agreements, and complexity are the sector's main IP strategies used in defence.

Innovation is systemic because there is a wide range of institutions, actors, and environmental factors that interact with one another in the process of innovating, in which elements of the process reinforce or weaken the system as they interact (Fagerberg and Godinho, 2006). In this sense, since defence is usually organized at a national level, it is necessary to observe the interconnections between private and public actors in a *systemic* way. Cristopher Freeman (1987, p. 1) introduces the concept of a national system of innovation (NSI) as 'the network of institutions in the public and private sectors whose activities and interactions initiate, import, modify and diffuse new technologies'. Furthermore, the so-called *triple-helix system*, developed by Ranga and Etzkowitz (2013), demonstrates that a triad among universities, government, and industry leads to a wider broader development of basic and applied science. The authors demonstrated empirically the positive correlation between the *triple-helix* and innovation.

The environmental aspect of innovation derives from the fact that actors and environment coevolve and interact. Actors calculate and formulate in different environmental settings. This varies significantly from early studies of innovation in neoclassical economic theory, which focused on equilibrium and technology as a public good and even recent discussions which treat actors as passive and dependent on exogenous factors. Innovation and, more specifically, cooperation, competition and inter-firm relations have a strong geographical aspect as well. Clusters of different industry segments are formed in regions (e.g., Brazil's São José dos Campos Aerospace Cluster). Rules and institutions (e.g., universities, public and private incentives) can be specific to sectors and regions. Thus, the notion of a sectoral system of innovation and production complements other concepts within the innovation system literature (Edquist, 1997).

In the case of defence products, variation in external threats, availability of substitute weapons, or changes in political willingness to purchase specific weapons aggravate uncertainty (Peck and Scherer, 1962). Hence, much of innovation studies and practices are centred around managing uncertainty. Innovation is highly difficult to explain or predict because of its contingent and systemic nature. When, through appropriability, the exploitation of economies of scale and scope are made possible, innovating is an extremely important vehicle for catching up, for both firms and countries. Those who lag behind lose important opportunities.

I started this work by focusing on the dependent variable and its main characteristics, which also provide clues about potential factors which impact innovation, both positively and negatively. However, as previously held, highly risk prone processes such as innovation, especially of the magnitude expected from large-scale defence projects, depend on a variety of economic issues, such as the relationship between the main actors involved, the constitution of an industrial base, and the specific traits of the defence market.

Furthermore, as a monopsonic demand market, procurement and incentives have great salience, as does the possibility of international collaboration and exportations. The budget arena is the core issue. Distribution of scarce resources determines the fate of large-scale projects in a given decision-making structure. These topics are now briefly discussed in order to better understand large-scale defence projects.

2.1.2 Market Structure

An innovative environment depends on a set of institutions, actors, and incentives which are systematically connected to create favourable conditions for technological transformations. In defence, building a solid DIB is crucial for success. In the past, the development of defence production came from the state's systematic coordination and international pressure (see Section 2.3). The development of economic relations in the civilian sector complemented the DIB. Especially since the Industrial Revolution, private firms have been able to produce at scale and enhance their participation in the sector, creating a web of various institutions. Although this has resulted in a rapid advancement of technological breakthroughs, some trade-offs must be highlighted: (i) private versus public productivity; (ii) internationalization versus national concerns; (iii) guns versus butter; (iv) R&D costs and benefits; (v) technological spin-off versus spin in; and (vi) the impacts of military spending. These issues are grounded in the production of defence equipment and thus the DIB. As such, they will be addressed briefly here. Some characteristics of the defence market are (i) the importance of R&D as a fixed cost; (ii) the importance of quantity, scale, and learning economies; and (iii) imperfect markets.

The US DIB was formalized in the 1950s, although one can argue that it has a strong inheritance from the structure of the Manhattan Project. The National Security Policy Council (NSC-68) directive was to support a build-up of US political, economic, and military strength (Watts, 2008). In the aftermath of the Second World War, the growing Soviet power had to be countered. The arms race in this case was highly demanding in terms of innovation. NSC-68/1 planned to double defence spending in two years. The United States aimed to develop nuclear submarines, aircraft carriers, ballistic missiles, jet aircraft, among others. The result was that the defence sector became the largest industrial sector of the US economy (Peck and Scherer, 1962).

A very important concept in defence economics is the DIB. The concept of DIB is not straightforward. Scholars usually understand it as the companies that provide defence equipment and materials with strategic objectives to the defence ministry. These products can be lethal large or small weapons systems – non-lethal but strategic products (e.g., vehicles, fuel, and infrastructure) and other products consumed by the military (e.g., food and clothing) (Dunne, 1995,

p. 402). Given this large scope and complex interconnectivity among different branches of production, it is often hard to define and map the DIB. Furthermore, firms can be the main contractors or subcontractors for large defence projects, they can be more civil or military oriented, and they can engage in international trade. These issues, among others, have led authors to restrict the concept of DIB to only those firms engaged directly in the development and production of goods and services specific to military engagement (Andrade, 2016; Sipri, 2020).

Some authors such as Amarante (2012) employ a broader approach to the concept.[3] The author argues that since war has become more technologically complex, an analysis of the DIB must include what is 'under the surface' of defence resource production, or what he calls the scientific-technological *Iceberg*.

The *Iceberg* concept includes not only the military product but also the logistics, production, conception, and R&D elements that surround the DIB. This holistic view of the DIB entails the need to include a wide variety of actors in the analysis, such as universities, engineering firms, industrial firms, service firms, technical teaching facilities, among others. Here I limit myself to adhering to the perspective of considering only arms systems with the sole purpose of engagement.

In accordance with the definition already adopted and proposing a more in-depth analysis, Walker et al., (1988) and Schofield (1993) suggest a taxonomy, which lists military products in a hierarchical manner ranging from the more complex defence oriented systems to the basic materials necessary for the production of defence equipment: (i) military strategies and concepts (high-level planning); (ii) integrated weapon and information systems (e.g., national early warning systems); (iii) major weapon platforms and communication systems (e.g., aircraft, battleships, and so on); (iv) complete weapon and communications component parts (e.g., torpedoes); (v) sub-systems (e.g., gyroscopes); (vi) sub-assemblies (e.g., sights and fuses); (vii) components (e.g., integrated circuits); and (viii) materials (e.g., semi-conductors). Adopting this taxonomy can provide a more precise identification of the firms that constitute the DIB. The industry considered here is specifically the one aimed at producing strictly for military engagement purposes. The focus is on items (i) to (iii), although it is necessary to state that in relation to large-scale projects (e.g., Manhattan), some components (uranium) are essential and, thus, complete analysis of some projects demand including a wider range of components.

Given the material structure of military production, a scholar of defence must investigate the material basis necessary to constitute a defence structure able tomobilize personnel and resources. It is necessary to point out the idiosyncrasies

---

[3] An interesting DIB concept is presented by the Brazilian ministry of defense as 'the group of firms, state or privately owned as well as the civil and military organizations who participate in the R&D, production, distribution and maintenance of strategic defense products' (BRASIL, 2005).

of the defence market, since these affect the other issues and problems in the sector. The first and foremost characteristic of the defence market is the state as the sole buyer. Governments' monopsonistic role determines the demand side of the market and affects the main features of the supply side as well. This has important implications for incentives and procurement, to be addressed next.

In the 1990s the supply side of the US DIB became extremely oligopolistic, through mergers and acquisitions (Watts, 2008). There are many entry barriers to the defence market such as a profound understanding of the political and acquisition process, close ties with the military, and willingness to invest in products that are difficult to convert to the civil sector. As a consequence, defence firms have developed historically in a particular way and the higher they move in the market hierarchy, the more the nature of capital equipment, labour skills, and the organization of production becomes specific to the sector. However, few competitors on the supply side may lead to economic inefficiency as well as exaggerated bargaining power of the contractors, characteristics which are expected to appear in more recent large-scale projects. Less competition has a negative effect on prices. Laffont and Tirole, (1993) demonstrated, through game theory analysis, that a small number of firms will engage in interactions with government, and this does not result in a socially desirable outcome. Asymmetrical information will affect the behaviour of the principal (buyer) and the agent (contractor), allowing contractors opportunities for both inefficiency and rents. An oligopolistic market structure also favours non-price forms of competition, which makes the design and production of the product more prone to delays, cost overruns, and technical problems. This requires major oversight of the government.

Market structure and its specific traits in defence raise important socio-economic questions such as the impacts and benefits of military spending. Besides the discussion about war and peace issues, the most controversial matter regarding the defence industry is its economic efficiency and effectiveness. The twentieth century witnessed a growing role assigned to government in providing basic services such as health and education, among others. Since government also acts as a provider of social benefits, military spending has been a target for criticism. This is most often known as the *guns versus butter* dilemma since there are opportunity costs for expenditure in other civilian sectors. Defence expenditure is an input measure. To measure outputs beyond the provision of a public good – security, strength, or deterrence – is a difficult task. There is no simple measure of benefits such as an equation which sums manpower and equipment. Security is not straightforward to measure. War depends on several unpredictable and non-pecuniary factors which can be neither predicted nor measured. Some examples include motivation, leadership, and mere luck (Clausewitz, 2007).

Twentieth-century engagements, for example, demonstrated that even in asymmetrical wars, the most developed country, both in terms of technology and manpower, may lose.

Given these issues, how is it possible to propose an adequate military expenditure input? Beyond the trade-offs presented, there is the question of the economic consequences of investing on the technological frontier. Authors diverge on this matter. Advocates of government investment in the military argue that it has beneficial impacts on the economy. These might include the provision of high-skill jobs, industrial planning, technological spin-offs, and solutions to underconsumption or overaccumulation crises (Diamond, 2006; Mowery, 2010). In contrast, other scholars highlight diversion and path dependence effects. Still other critics have observed that the DIB crowds out resources in both investment and human capital efforts, reduces civil technological development, and has externality effects on other companies (Dunne, 1995). Consequently, it has reduced industrial efficiency and international competitiveness.

Moreover, since the 1980s, economists have observed that, differently from the past *spin-offs* resultant from mobilizing efforts, innovation has been characterized by a *spin-in* effect towards the defence sector, in other words, technology is flowing from the commercial/civil sector to the DIB. Another important issue is that O&M and personnel expenditures have grown continuously as a share of defence input. This rise in cost relative to procurement expenditure has led to pressure to reduce resources which are the main source of revenue for the DIB. Similar to *spin-in* technological effects is the fact that the private sector is providing growing appeal as a career choice for the most qualified engineers and researchers. This is a result of the government losing its ability to control and access technology (Watts, 2008). Such changes give procurement regulation, process optimizing, and the provision of incentives for innovation in the DIB great importance.

2.1.3 Procurement and Incentives

In a monopsonic demand scenario, the government exercises its market power especially through procurement and incentives. Authors are increasingly arguing that innovation and *spin-offs* as possible outcomes of government military expenditures are diminishing. The most appropriate way to stimulate innovation from the procedural perspective is through procurement and incentives. The main problem is that efficient use of equipment, in theoretical terms, resembles a market scenario, where optimization is achieved through adjustments in a competitive profit-seeking environment. In the defence market, however, as stated by Sandler and Hartley (1995), the absence of competition and the nature of employment contracts do not drive cost minimization. In other words, in defence, cost function does not make components cheaper. Incentives for efficiency are therefore diminished. Several authors have argued that the major prime contractors, the Armed Forces, Defence Departments, and interest groups have vested interests in lobbying governments and affecting the competitive process in procurement. Influence groups use, for example, arguments such as job creation, and allocating production to marginal constituencies. In the literature, this is usually referred to as the military industrial complex, following the famous speech of President Eisenhower (1961).

As a topic that will be further developed in Section 2.3, incentives are additionally dampened by parochial bureaucratic interests, and thus, political disputes distort potential cost and performance standards. In this regard, Rogerson (1995) argues that since objective measures of military performance are hard to attain, Congress has strong incentives not to delegate decision-making and, consequently, the works towards controlling and managing the process. By scrutinization of officials, budgetary control and political opposition, Congress in the United States exercises a strong role in defence. This is not the case in other countries such as Brazil, where military expenditures and interests are almost entirely delegated to the Armed Forces.

The DoD can exert its power in procurement by controlling the early stages of development and demanding the often complex and hard-to-scrutinize specificities of the weapon systems. Annual appropriations by Congress, therefore, compel stakeholders to make difficult technical decisions which will affect the budget in the forthcoming years. Innovation is highly risky and defence equipment might have a lifecycle of forty years. Thus, decisions are made in scenarios of great uncertainty. 'Huge uncertainties pervade the process and complete long-term contracts are generally impossible to write and difficult to enforce' (Rogerson, 1995, p. 311). Therefore, cost–benefit analysis must take into consideration rivalling equipment in terms of its life cycle costs, including maintenance and operation of the total fleet. Furthermore, strategic implications and military features of the equipment compared to the alternatives and even international market alternatives are part of the cost analysis and political disputes in procurement (Rogerson, 1995). A major source of pressure that the DoD can wield on stakeholders is their specialized knowledge of war engagement and advocacy for the need to purchase determined equipment. It is hard for a Congress member to take on risks regarding security, and therefore, they have to count on a body of specialists as well. Furthermore, the military can induce Congress to choose higher-quality technologies and in larger quantities, as they present options with low decrease in marginal cost but that require large-scale production.

Industry is in between Congress and the military in the procurement process. As argued by Hartley (1995), in making proposals, they might take a purely objective approach, giving priority to costs, performance, and delivery. The wider economic and industrial benefits are a task for the senior players. In the procurement process per se, decisions will also be influenced by constituency, job, re-election, and other considerations. These concerns are incorporated into senior player's interest-maximizing behaviour, as I argue in Section 2.3. The problem arises, therefore, in building a consensus which will mitigate the interests of profit-seeking and highly specialized firms and stakeholders to reach an appropriate 'defence output'.

The type of products in which a defence firm invests raises a series of problems for them. Especially nowadays, projects are extremely expensive and complex, and there is a substantial investment in developing a proposal. Losing a major contract is thus a major setback for the firm. One issue mentioned throughout this Element is the problem of conversion. The highly specific nature of defence products can hardly be transposed into civil goods. Furthermore, as argued by Hartley (1995), R&D expenses on defence privilege performance over cost and, therefore, make the products less marketable in the civil sector. Another major issue concerning cost-efficiency of military production is the optimization of capital investment and production facilities. This affects both the demand and the supply side of the defence market since both will lose with plant closures and job losses.

Firms worry that they will never recover their expenses which are usually very specific to a particular project and thus require investment in physical capital and professionals that cannot easily be employed in different projects. As a result, government's main stakeholders concede different forms of guarantees to the investing firms to assure the incentive for innovation. Firstly, the government, different from typical commercial consumers, funds the value of the R&D investment, as well as the final product. Also, after winning the competition, the firm is awarded 'follow-on revenue' non-competitive contracts, which account for the majority of the firm's gains. Non-competitive contracts can increase the profit margin of firms in comparison to profits in the commercial market since contracting firms are able to transfer overhead and pension costs of their commercial operations to government. This results in disproportional profit compared with civil commercial activities.

Competition is usually harsh fierce during the design phase, where a single winner is chosen based on the design's projected performance, cost, and maintainability issues. The contract is most commonly awarded to a single firm due to economies of scale. Large-scale projects typically have no close substitute and thus competition is limited and winning a major contract may mean a large share of a firm's potential market. The effects of lack of competition and the ultimate monopolistic role played by the winning firm are usually countered by legislation, which determines that the price includes historic and projected accounting costs which are meticulously audited. After the contract is awarded, a set of targets are to be achieved by the project.

Generally speaking, economies more directed to trade liberalization are open to direct foreign investment and trade. In defence, however, especially given security concerns and highly sensitive technological advances, a *trade-off* between a more internationalized procurement and production process and a more nationalistic one is presented. Large-scale defence projects have high costs and technological difficulties, which could be mitigated through international collaboration avoiding duplication of costly R&D programs. Furthermore, marginal costs would fall, because of scale production. A more orthodox economic perspective within the literature points to the promotion of comparative advantages that would result from international specialization from more open defence markets, decreasing industry costs. Regarding the balance of payments, while defenders of protectionism emphasize the deficit problem, adherents of a more pro-market perspective argue that international division of labour would enhance welfare, and, as a result, create jobs and allocate resources to productive sectors of the economy. The arguments mentioned can be identified with two extremes: a country's choice to completely open the defence market or to purchase all equipment and technology domestically. Between these extremes, several possibilities arise. Defence industry collaboration is not accomplished naturally among contenders and thus the debate revolves around alliances (e.g., NATO) and partnerships. More radical options, such as a centralized procurement office 'purchasing common equipment offer the greatest cost savings but, politically, it is the most difficult to implement' (Hartley, 1995, P. 468). However, different options present themselves in relation to the type of product. Those that are highly sensitive, for example, sharing nuclear technology and delivery vessels are practically out of the question. The United States has, however, counted on exports to allies and partners, and this has, therefore, enhanced its DIB in times of relative peace. Oscillations in defence spending, procurement, and its incentives affect a firm's strategies and the tendency to look for international markets. From 1970 to 1976, at the advent of the *détente*, for example, foreign defence sales in the top twenty-five US defence firms 'rose from under 4 percent of the revenues to over 20' (Watts, 2008, p. 23). I do not deny possible benefits of both collaboration for new projects and exportations, but I stand in agreement with Hartley (1995, p. 475) that

the armed forces, bureaucracies, contractors and scientists within each partner nation will insist upon imposing their requirements, ideas and technical
aspirations. Bargaining is inevitable. At the start of the program, each partner
nation's armed forces will insist upon their operational requirements; firms
will compete for project leadership; and each country's scientists will demand
to be involved in the most exciting technical advances.

Large-scale defence projects are of great political and economic importance
since they are the pillars of resource mobilization and allocation strategy, and
their success or failure carries significant weight for a country's future position.
Sensitive technology, interstate competition, uncertainty about the future of the
project, and parochial and bureaucratic interests are some of the features that
further complicate decision-making. Regarding alliances, even though some are
lasting and enduring, it would be highly risky, given history, and even recent
history, to transfer sensitive technology to other countries. Although the case of
the F-35 counted on international collaboration, the rules and the process were
controlled by its leading producer. As argued in Section 2.2, alliances are
a function of elements, which cannot be relied on in the long run. A country,
ultimately, must depend on its own efforts to enhance its competitive power.

Countries lacking the necessary futures for innovating on their own, however,
must rely on purchasing equipment from *off the shelf* markets or work in
collaboration with other firms to provide assets that they cannot produce on
their own. This is the case with Brazil and its F-X and KC-390 programs, for
example. Variables such as low investment, low R&D, no guarantee of demand,
among others, affect the options for producing national technology. Firms in
Brazil must usually seek *dual-use* production. Furthermore, these companies
must rely on export to achieve the necessary scale to recover their investments.
Oscillations in defence spending, procurement, and incentives affect the firm's
strategies and their tendency to look for international markets.

As I have pointed out, central marks of a project's development have been
chosen to facilitate the analysis. The lifecycle of a project is also subject to
complex legislation and sets of rules. The next section briefly outlines these
issues. However, highly specific rules regarding the procurement processes are
not the subject of investigation. Instead, only the general process is outlined.
The focus is on the centrality of the budgetary arena, since it is where the
proposed independent variables reveal their true impact and interrelations.

2.1.4 Budgeting Is Politics

Budgeting is at the centre of defence economics and encompasses the variables
that I propose in this Element. The dispute among resources ultimately reveals
a winning or losing coalition, arguments about external threat and their urgency,

and the possibility of responding with defence projects. Among structure, actors, and issues, a quintessential process presents itself and encompasses them all: the budget. In budgeting, the structure and the main actors appear in a sense that their role can be inferred. Furthermore, economic trade-offs and strategic and tactical considerations are considered in the arguments of stakeholders and the decision-making process in a more objective way. There is no policy without resource mobilization and allocation. 'The victories and defeats, the compromises and the bargains, the realms of agreement and the spheres of conflict regarding the role of national government in our society all appear in the budget. In the most integral sense, the budget lies at the heart of the political process' (Wildavsky, 1964, p. 5). Achieving political objectives through national security policy without a correspondent budget is merely a political rhetoric.

Adams and Williams (2010, p. 222) hold that when analysing national security issues, the literature rarely engages with this important matter: 'Analysts of the national security policymaking rarely dig into the politics of the budgetary process.' As I show in Section 2.3, incrementalism generally prevails in the budget. That is to say, there are no substantial fluctuations from year to year. There has been considerable progress by scholars in explaining exceptions. In defence spending, budget fluctuations are usually correlated to external threat and war. However, since I address specific large-scale projects, it is important to state that individual programs do not follow the same logic.

Demarest (2017) maintains that, contrary to expectations, budget outcomes are frequently volatile and unpredictable at the individual program level. This is a crucial point since in this Element, I propose budgetary volatility as a parameter to explain the success of failure of a large-scale project. According to Demarest (2017, p. 12): 'program funding is markedly non-incremental (...) individual program funding fluctuates wildly as political and programmatic battles are won and lost, contrary to the conventional portrait of an immovable budget'. Congressional authorizing and appropriating committees modify funding requests substantially in the case of individual programs, as seen in the comparative case study sections of this Element. According to Demarest, overall budget can be largely explained by external threat. It is the political factors and economic development structure, however, that can explain budget fluctuations in specific cases and scenarios.

Strategy in defence policy has a political aim. A good strategy has to constrain parochial interests in the sense that, in a democratic state, it achieves a balance between interest groups and military–civil relations. The process and organizational/institutional arrangements outlined in this section are a complex and schematic representation of the attempts in the United States to achieve this balance, especially since Secretary McNamara's initiatives in the 1960s. In the United States, Secretary of Defence Robert McNamara, who served from 1961 to 1968, appointed Charles Hitch as controller for the Office of the Secretary of Defense (OSD) to implement the Planning, Programming, and Budgeting System (PPBS), as soon as 1961, in the Pentagon's annual budget. The Executive began to analyse cost-effectiveness in order to choose among weapon programs. Furthermore, firms were obligated to provide the government with detailed cost information about their activities. Recent important developments occurred at the beginning of this century, including DoD Directive 5000.02 (January, 2020). These initiatives were an attempt to improve and update the PPBS, which was renamed as Planning, Programming, Budgeting and Execution (PPBE), to emphasize the execution phase as a priority. Furthermore, under Secretary of Defense Donald Rumsfeld, the Joint Capabilities Integration and Development System (JCIDS) was introduced (2003), which redefined acquisition requirements and evaluation criteria for defence programs. The concept of *spiral innovation*, which will be addressed in the Future Combat System case study, was introduced in these directives. It consists of simultaneous employment of technological development, feedback, and further enhancement of the system.

Congress holds the 'power of the purse'. Key congressional committees (House Armed Service Committee, Senate Armed Service Committee, Senate Acquisition Committee, and House Acquisition Committee), alongside auditing agencies and hearings can substantially influence the funding of a project. Thus, the need to approve the presidential budget entails building a consensus among the senior players and balancing parochial interests. Beyond these committees, other actors and processes are extremely important in the budgetary process. I reiterate, however, that they are only discussed here in general terms.[4]

2.1.5 Technological Feasibility

Technological feasibility – the possibility of accomplishing the project's objectives – is a necessary condition for the success of high-scale defence projects. Throughout its lifecycle, a project's prospects of maturing and demonstrating technological feasibility affect the stakeholder's position in defence of or in opposition to the project. Firstly, as already stated, innovation is risk. The projects dealt with here reflect the technological frontier, determined by stakeholder's need, external threat, and the objective of the bureaucracies involved to enhance their power. However, it is impossible to know ex ante whether a project will work. Nonetheless, as the project advances through its

---

[4] For a detailed assessment of the budgetary process in the United States, see Adams and Williams, 2010; Candreva, 2017.

lifecycle, with scrutinization by specialists and Congress, the perspectives for a feasible product become clearer. At a given time, feasibility can be accessed through proxy parameters.

Theoretically, a solid industrial base, efficient procurement, and incentives working through a budgetary system optimize the distribution of scarce resources and facilitate technological feasibility. Stakeholders can affect the technological feasibility prospects of a project by granting resources. The main point is that, as I show in the case studies, government is authorized to change, reduce, or cancel a project during its development. Technological feasibility issues are at the core of the problem, since failing to deliver to the needs of performance and cost demands of the *senior players*[5] diminishes a project's strength. There is no precise measurement available to assess technological feasibility, especially in new, state-of-the-art projects. However, in times of a disputed budget, stakeholders do not grant further resources to a project with cost uncertainties and immature technologies. The amount allocated to the project is therefore volatile in proportion to its prospects and other budgetary demands. As I argue, there is a constant pulling and hauling among bureaucracies and *senior players*, and the result determines the resources mobilized for the project.

Incentives, procurement, accessing international markets, and the impacts of military expenditure are some of the factors that affect decision-making. They are embedded, however, in the efficiency and effectiveness of the project's outcome. When the government endorses technological mobilization and resource allocation to the defence sector, it means the project is doing well during its lifecycle. As I argue, technological feasibility responds to and is correlated with external threats since the government dedicates more resources to defence. The more resources, the more likely it is that the project will work. In the same way, stakeholders and senior players, especially when faced with the need for the project and backed by a minimum consensus of parochial interests, support the program, and grant the necessary resources. On the other hand, tight budgets and other parochial interests, and budgetary priorities, make the project likely to be halted. If stakeholders, together with specialists and specialized agencies (e.g., CBO, Congressional Research Service (CRS), and GAO), determine that the technological challenges in the current phase of the project are not worth it, the project fails. Thus, one way to assess technological feasibility in a proxy manner is through volatility of the budget that stakeholders assign to the project.

---

[5] Concept is further addressed and developed in Section 3. To put it briefly, *senior players* hold positions that can affect defence acquisition and budget. Their needs, therefore, are here considered a Success Criteria.

2.1.6 Data and Hypothesis

In this Element, I argue that there are some proxy measures to be analysed when reconstructing the history of the development of a project. Throughout its lifecycle, assessments of technological feasibility are made by specialists and subject to scrutiny. These qualitative indicators are introduced alongside measures like the difference among the unit and total cost estimates, procurement quantity reductions, and the volatility of demand for the project in question. The elasticity of the demand is a strong indicator of the prospects for the project. If demand is too volatile, in both quantity and cost, the project is facing trouble. This works as a proxy parameter for technological feasibility. These measures are affected by, and impact senior player positions, and ultimately define the outcome of the project. Persistent challenges and doubts surrounding the project weaken it. Considering the indicators cited, the main hypothesis regarding technological feasibility is:

> Between t1 and t2 or tn ... for example, the variation of demand, in both quantity and cost, is a strong indicator of the project's technological feasibility. Furthermore, the higher the difference between the projected cost (unitary and total) and schedule and the real cost and schedule, the more likely the project is to face technological feasibility problems.

Measurement and analysis of the project in an ex-post scenario can be subject to criticism in the sense that it might become tautological. However, as I argue here, innovation is systemic and evolutionary, and there is a constant change in the political and external environment scenario. Feasibility affects the project during its whole lifecycle and changes according to resource availability, among others factors. Analysing feasibility from this perspective can provide important evidence to support the development of the model.

2.2 External Threat, Constraint, and Innovation

Innovation in defence, as stated previously, poses a challenge in terms of the choice of variables for analysis. However, as it is considered a strategic industry and its outcome is to provide security, omitting relevant causal factors which motivate and pressure states to innovate and compete would seriously compromise the efforts to develop a theoretical framework such as the one proposed here. Although in the model I propose in this Element, the independent variables are interrelated in a systemic manner, the analysis requires that initially they be treated separately. I now address the impacts of the International System on the state's responses and its effects on innovation.

To better assess the impacts of the International System at the state level, some theories have been advanced. Since this section is dedicated exclusively to the international sources of state behaviour, it is appropriate to focus on the neorealist theory, as it offers the most systematic and theoretically solid approach to the subject. Neorealist theory postulates that states are constrained by the International System to balance against one another in order to survive, regardless of their objectives. States are 'trapped' in a 'security dilemma', which compels them to arm themselves since their neighbours, in a context of suspicion, will do the same. The theory assumes the structure as anarchic, with functional equivalency among the units (states). These premises lead to the conclusion that the only thing that changes in the International System is the distribution of power and polarity, that is – the number of great powers. States are expected to balance and enhance their capabilities. Other perspectives develop upon or dialogue systematically with neorealist theoretical insights. I claim that the best way of translating the imperatives of the International System into an independent variable which affects large-scale innovative projects in defence is through threat level.

2.2.1 Theory of International Politics

Neorealist theory was put forward by Kenneth Waltz (1979) in his seminal work *Theory of International Politics*. Since then, much of the debate within the discipline of International Relations has centred around his work. He proposes a systemic theory in which a political structure is understood to comprise the organizing principle of a system, the differentiation of functional units, and the distribution of capabilities across units (Waltz, 1979). In this formulation, what characterizes the International System is anarchy, functional equivalency of the units (as opposed to on the domestic level), and distribution of power among units. As long as anarchy prevails, the only possible form of structural change is the distribution of capabilities among units.

Derived from Waltz's theory is a system where the structure imposes on states the responsibility of self-help. In an anarchic environment, the sine qua non condition for any aspiration is survival. The consequence of anarchy is a competitive and insecure arena that pervades the life of the states. This logic underlies the *security dilemma* (Herz, 1950). Herz argues that, in order to survive, states attempt to surpass adversaries generating a similar response. The consequence is an arms race among contenders, in a spiral logic. Following this line of inference, to survive, states are impelled to enhance their capabilities, as they are suspicious of other states' intentions. The primary path of building capabilities is through military means to ensure physical survival, a precondition for other forms of competition. Systemic pressure, however, does not determine state behaviour, but constrains it. Since state behaviour cannot be precisely predicted (Waltz, 1996), systemic pressure does not result in automatic balancing behaviour. Although, in parallel with firm theory, if a state fails to respond to systemic imperatives, it can, in an extreme scenario, cease to exist.

States can respond to the constraints imposed by the International System by *balancing*. In his formulation of balancing, Waltz argues that a state can balance in two main ways: (i) external balancing; and (ii) internal balancing. The first refers to the state seeking to strengthen and enlarge its alliance or to weaken and shrink an opposing one. The second is the way the state strengthens through internal efforts by enhancing its material and military capabilities. External balancing has been well developed in IR theory.

My focus in this Element is on internal balancing as it more clearly correlates with the issues addressed.

2.2.2 Systemic Pressure and Development of Capabilities

As shown, it is expected that state behaviour may be explained through structural incentives and constraints imposed by the International System. Self-help and competition compel states to enhance their power either by forming alliances to balance other states or by strengthening their material capabilities and improving their strategies. Other potential forms of behaviour are engaging in buck-passing or *band wagoning* (free ride).

Waltz did not develop a theory of internal balancing. Nonetheless, authors believe that such a theory is believed to be latent in Waltz's formulation. Resende-Santos (2007), among others, attempted to fill this gap by presenting systematic analysis and theoretical building on the subject. According to Resende-Santos, internal balancing can be achieved either by emulation, innovation, or countermeasuring. Three dimensions constitute military internal balancing behaviour: organizational, doctrinal, and technological. States can emulate, countermeasure, or innovate targeted practices for each of these dimensions; juxtapose them in a combination; or choose to emulate partially or fully the one that is most successful.

Studies have been published on long-lasting military organizational emulations, military responses to external constraints, and balancing behaviour targeted at specific dimensions of military response. Figure 2 presents the main potential state balancing responses to international constraints. In this Element, I focus and concentrate on internal balancing, more specifically, the innovative technological dimension. Moreover, this work focuses mainly on innovation and innovative-capable states, as it attempts to explain the United States' cutting-edge defence transformations. States innovate if they have a margin of security which permits them to do so, since they must maintain regular military operations while assuming the inherent risk of innovating. This occurs mostly, but not exclusively, with great powers (Resende-Santos, 2007).

Gourevitch (1978) developed a thesis according to which the internal behaviour of states is determined by external constraints. According to the author (Gourevitch, 1978, p. 883), a state's political development is shaped by war and trade. Gourevitch argues that anarchy poses a threat which can result in occupation, annihilation, or the reduction to the status of subserviency. The above of threat, according to Gourevitch (1978), is opportunity in the form of power, dominion, glory, and security.

This perspective is endorsed by authors in the field of historical sociology, such as Nobert Elias (1993) and Charles Tilly (1990), who study the *sociogenesis* of modern states. By their reasoning, the pressure of war requires small units to prepare or be subjugated. A dynamic process induces an expansionist behaviour of political units. 'The soul preservation in social existence requires, in free competition, a permanent expansion. Who doesn't rise, falls' (Elias, 1993, p. 134). A similar line of argument can be found in John Mearsheimer's neorealist theory of great power competition. Mearsheimer (2014, p. 2) argues that 'the desire for more power does not go away, unless a state achieves the ultimate goal of hegemony'.

Figure 3 represents the options available to states when faced with systemic constraints. They have the option of enhancing their internal capabilities by emulation, innovation, countermeasuring, or simply maintaining their current course. Great powers will have more incentive to innovate. These can be targeted, full scale, or partial, and they comprise technological, doctrinal, and organizational spheres. States also have the option to buck-pass (*free-ride*) and transfer their costs. Bandwagoning is mostly a strategy of weak and vulnerable states, and it refers to aligning to a great power. Formal alliance making is the essence of balancing, but it is important to state that alliances are volatile, especially in systems where there are three or more contenders. This theory is by no means complete. It assumes states as passive actors responding to systemic stimuli, which can foster many criticisms from those who assume that domestic variables have more causal weight in determining state behaviour.

This far I have critically focused on demonstrating the causal weight of the systemic imperatives towards states' behaviour. As a dynamic process, external imperatives directly affect the state's modernization requirements. Deriving from a neorealist perspective, Resende-Santos (2007, pp. 64–65) summarizes this logic as follows: 'competitive effectiveness is structurally determined. It is not a quality of the individual units, but a product of their competition (...) the anarchic structure alone determines the minimum requirements of viability in the system'. I argue that it is not the structure alone; although it has causal weight, economic and political domestic variables have to be taken into account.

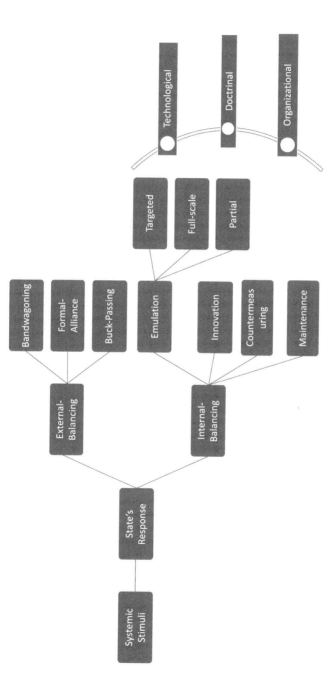

Figure 3 Military balancing options

Source: Dall'Agnol, 2022, p. 42.

Gourevitch proposes translating systemic pressure into domestic economic and political organization as follows: 'this state of war induces states to organize themselves internally so as to meet these external challenges' (1978, p. 896). I hold that the anarchic structure of the International System forces states to constantly innovate. The systemic approach provides us with general predictions and rules but does not contribute to explaining specific large-scale defence projects, although it can be very useful when explaining long-term innovative endeavours. To assess the nuances of successful or unsuccessful projects, however, one must translate systemic pressure into an operational variable and employ an interdisciplinary approach.

I argue that the level of threat has casual significance in determining state behaviour, especially in defence. Defence policy is the most easily identified channel in states' response to the International System. The question is how to operationalize an independent systemic variable to present a more objective relation between the structure and state response. What differentiates states in the International System is their relative position in the distribution of power. Systemic features materialize objectively before a state as threats. Beyond distribution of power or, in other words, relative distribution of material capabilities, direct threat and general *longue durée* competition also affect innovative cutting-edge technological developments. The next section addresses these issues in more detail.

2.2.3 Threat, Innovation, and Large-Scale Defence Projects

As already mentioned, states facing external pressures derived from the anarchic structure can engage in external balancing and internal balancing. While the literature focuses mainly on external balancing, I endorse Resende-Santos' (2007) argument that a state may be fortunate in having generous friends and external circumstances, but ultimately it must count on its own efforts and strength.

Since the main purpose of this Element is to propose a systemic model subject to testing, it is necessary to emphasize that the purpose of theory is to generate a testable and useful framework to simplify complex phenomena. In this sense, the arbitrary choice of variables is inevitable, be the study parsimonious or idiosyncratic. Attempting to incorporate all possible variables that carry some sort of causal weight would require the analysis to incorporate an immense quantity of independent and intervenient variables,[6] as some theories of foreign policy and public policy do. Instead of making analysis more precise, this can be detrimental for the purposes of explaining or understanding.

---

[6] Intervenient variables affect the relation between the Independent Variable and the Dependent Variable. Thus, for example, pressure affects the temperature water will boil.

The main problem of inferring a causal relationship derived from systemic pressure towards explaining state behaviour and, by consequence, the nuances of public policy, is measurement. The level of threat is proposed in this study as an independent variable explaining the outcomes of the large defence projects. The literature does not present a precise measuring standard for the level of threat. As threat is correlated to relative distribution of power, relative capabilities may be considered determinants of threat. Rough estimates to measure capabilities are found in the literature (Waltz, 1979) – generally the sum of economic resources, population, territory, and military assets. Therefore, the level of threat is usually dealt with in a qualitative manner, thus presenting a complicated obstacle to variable operationalization. Resende-Santos (2007) argues that IR lacks a theory of threat, a very difficult concept to operationalize.

Theories that propose threat as a variable for state behaviour, such as that put forward by Walt (1987), usually rely on factors such as perception, aggressive intentions, and geography. Perceptions and intentions are far from useful for theoretical construction if the intention is to build a generalizable model. As for geography, its direct effect on state behaviour is undeniable for example, British maritime strategy as opposed to Germany's land strategy. However, if the purpose is to achieve a more objective measure, the theory must rely on a *ceteris paribus* condition regarding these factors. Systematic separation of intentions and capabilities as components of threat is not possible since the former is usually materialized only in the light of the latter. These elements do not have to be included as components of the level of threat, since they alter primarily the *type of threat* and the characteristics of *states' response*. Regardless of this effect, in theoretical terms, one can reasonably assume that this does not change the direct positive relation between threat and innovation in general terms.

The position of the state in the system's distribution of power demonstrates the objective level of threat. Specific traits like geography or perception may be useful in deeper analysis of specific cases but are detrimental to a more theoretical systematic framework of analysis in terms of research methodology. Nonetheless, as argued, direct threat and a *longue durée* systemic pressure also affect state-building and, as a consequence, innovation. These variables can be assessed through *proxy* parameters and complemented with qualitative analysis and comparison among case studies. The relation between systemic pressure and innovation is well characterized by Resende-Santos:

> All competitive realms have built-in incentives for innovating, since the prospective payoffs of successful innovation are great. Emulation may bring security payoffs, but the payoffs from successful innovation are likely

to be greater (...) The international system, like the market, generates ceaseless technical and organizational innovation. The system is in constant motion because of it. (2007, p. 72)

The relation between threat and innovation is direct and positive. Faced with threats, states have greater incentive to engage in innovative balancing behaviour. The system's pressure and constraints on state behaviour also enhance innovative pace and scale in a causal positive relation. In the long run, I argue, this holds true regarding specific large-scale defence projects. When faced with a direct and imminent threat, stakeholders also value innovation, especially through budgets.

In this regard, a hypothesis put forward by Elman (1999) and Posen (1984) maintains that in the face of imminent threat, states are compelled to centralize decision-making in defence. As a result, the chain of command becomes more rigid and integrated. This allows decision-makers to adequately counter the growing threat by mobilizing and distributing resources and mitigating possible interorganizational conflicts and interests. I argue here that in the face of imminent and direct threat, stakeholders grant resources to innovative projects. The relation between direct threat and innovation is positive. Specific projects, however, can be subject to bureaucratic interests and pulling and hauling. Although for theoretical purposes this relation can be supported, as interorganizational conflicts and the interests associated with stakeholders are not necessarily attenuated. I claim here that there is a direct and positive impact of threat in innovation, although it is not a necessary condition for its success. As stated by Clausewitz 'force, to counter opposing force, equips itself with the inventions of art and science' (2007, p. 13). Technology has its limits and there are human factors in war, which may be decisive.

Two other relevant aspects must be developed before concluding this section. Firstly, states have a range of balancing options such as the pursuit of alliances or buck-passing, for example. In this study, I endorse Resende-Santos' position already presented. Ultimately, states have to rely on their own efforts. However, balancing options can influence states' responses both in qualitative and quantitative manners. This might affect the level of innovation, although this relation is not addressed here. Furthermore, regardless of this effect, in theoretical terms, it is reasonable to assume that the direct positive relation between threat and innovation in general terms does not change. Resende-Santos (2007) holds that a state will innovate beyond the regular defence activities for which it is responsible while it has a margin of safety. As a result, the most innovative-capable states are great powers. I believe that a state with a low threat level at a given time can still innovate in the face of a growing threat. This is the case because threat level growth is relative and not absolute. Consequently, even facing growing threats, nothing apparently dictates that states will cease to have the extra margin of safety and resources that makes them innovatively capable.

Finally, it is argued that these projects are the material backbone of many cases of innovative internal balancing behaviour. I maintain that in a *ceteris paribus* scenario, threat will have a directly proportional relation with innovation, as it is the most structural incentive. As more resources and stakeholders' attention and urgency are devoted to counter such a threat, in the case of no immediately available substitutes and the project demonstrating itself technologically feasible, the greater the threat, the more likely the project is to succeed.

2.2.4 Data and Hypothesis

There are many options of variables in the study of defence economics. Engaging in theory always involves the risk of oversimplifying. Nonetheless, when attempting to explain the success and failure of large-scale projects, the analyst cannot risk omitting a variable such as external threat, with its potential causal weight.

The main hypothesis put forward here is that 'innovative-capable states innovate in the military sphere in a directly proportional relation to the level of threat measured in terms of the relative distribution of power. Hence, ceteris paribus, the greater the threat level, the more likely an innovation is to succeed. Large-scale projects, as the technological pillars of innovation, are more likely to succeed in the face of a high level of threat'.

It was argued that the relative distribution of material capabilities is the most precise measure to objectively access threat. Correlates of War offers an index, which aggregates capabilities to measure distribution of power. The greater the relative capabilities, the lower the threat level. The same source also created an index based on the interstate military disputes, which works as a direct threat database, but only complemented with qualitative analysis. A thorough investigation is needed of the cases since the database only represents a very specific aspect of threat. This holds because interstate disputes do not necessarily represent large threats, but represent conflict escalation among states. Defence expenditure also works as a *proxy* variable for evaluating direct threat, since it is constantly being modified according to specific contingencies. However, this does not apply for specific projects, or subcomponents of expenditure. Hence, it also has to be analysed in the light of the other parameters and sources. As for the cited *longue durée* incidence between state-building and innovation, the analysis is qualitative, since it is built upon a historical perspective presented by some authors, such as Tilly (1990) and Ellias (1993). Nonetheless, military expenditure can give insights regarding systemic long duration pressure. State-building in this sense involves several other elements, for example economic development and taxation. A variation of threat, presented in both quantitative and qualitative modes, can be scored from low to high in the analysis of a project.

Figure 4 refers to the relative distribution of material capabilities. I claim that it has a direct relation with innovation in general and is positively related to the success of innovative projects. The score relates to the percentage that a country holds of the world's key material capabilities. Several parameters, for example territory and population, were incorporated by the COW project to create the index. The data cover most of lifecycles of the projects selected for analysis. Since it is an ongoing and recent project, recent developments in the F-35 will have to be assessed by other means. The lower the percentage (Y axis) in the relative distribution of power, the greater the threat the states face.

Figure 4 represents the relative distribution of material capabilities, in the form of a *proxy* elaborated by the COW project. The Y axis is the proportion of key strategic components that the United States held across time. The higher the control of these assets, the more powerful and safe the country is. It is important to point out that it does not take into consideration regional, geographical, and direct threat dimensions. In the early 1990s and mid-2000s, the United States had a considerable amount of the relative distribution of power, according to Figure 4. The years of the late 1970s were considered to be a period of relative decline in US power, with discussions about the end of its hegemony. To

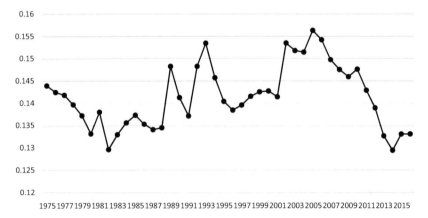

Figure 4 Relative distribution of material capabilities
Source: Correlates of War, 2023. The author.

external threat, I attribute a score from low to high based on the relative distribution of power.

Direct threat is hard to assess. As argued, it must rely on a *ceteris paribus* condition concerning perception and geography, among other factors through several escalation scores. One might think that a threat posed by China, for example, and a hypothetical capacity to reach the US territory is higher than a greater escalation in the Middle East, for example. That is endorsed here. Direct threat will be only assessed qualitatively, addressing the way it affects the specific large-scale project, as it is the case with the FCS and the wars on the Middle East, for example.

In addition to issues of data, I argue that regarding the dimensions of innovation presented, technology has causal linear preponderance in relation to organization and doctrine, since substantial variation in the former can compel states to adjust to the latter. Although I believe it is not a *necessary* condition for a specific project to meet the SC presented, I agree that systemic imperatives, translated into threat, compel states to both nation-building and innovation. Pace, scale, and timing of innovation are related to the level of threat. The higher the threat, the more innovation assumes greater speed, scale, and urgency. Innovative capable states (great powers) are the main innovators, but this does not preclude in any way the possibility of other states innovating, even if only in specific military economic sectors.

2.3 Decision-Making, Defence, and the Domestic Arena

Although, as already previously, the success of large-scale defence projects is strongly correlated to threat level and requires technological feasibility within the economic/innovative structure, accurate decision-making is also necessary. Decisions usually revolve around a structure, its main actors, processes, and issues. The decision-making theories and processes outlined can be applied to different issues. I present here some of the main elements proposed to explain decision-making. I do not adhere fully to them, although propositions are mainly derived from bureaucratic politics (BP) theory. I argue that a minimum degree of consensus among and within the Executive and Congress, in the case of the United States, is a *necessary* condition for the success of large-scale defence projects. This consensus must, at least, provide material resources for the project's advancement. Various interests, such as bureaucratic ones and the availability of resources for projects that stakeholders consider necessary, may moderate these efforts. The conclusions so far hold true: imminent threats, technical challenges, and sufficient opposing pressure affect consensus building around the project.

2.3.1 Bounded Rationality and Theoretical Building

Since its establishment as a distinct field, political science has engaged in a fundamental question: who decides? Who rules and who obeys? Furthermore, decisions vary according to issues, the process of deciding and the constraints of ruling, due to both external and internal factors. The choice of actors is thus of extreme importance. Even when one attempts to build a solid methodological approach, arbitrariness is inevitable in the choice of variables. Proof of such an assertion is the immense number of independent variables used by researchers to investigate public policy. Beyond that, studies vary in terms of the level of analysis – international, domestic, and sub-national – and units of analysis – individuals, groups, and coalitions. Building a model that incorporates all levels of analysis, relevant actors, and issues, for example, in the form of a matrix, would be so extensive and complicated that it would lose all its explanatory power. Furthermore, studies which attempt such an endeavour usually incur profound epistemological and ontological incompatibilities. In this section, I propose a debate engaging with some fundamental theories and justify the choice to opt for some propositions to the detriment of others.

While investigating the case of presidential democracies, the extent of the president's power is indispensable for analysis. If a state's response to external threat or its decision to innovate relies on presidential decision and assumptions of instrumental rationality and maximizing outputs, decisions would not deviate unless some 'mistake' was made. Nonetheless, a first wave of scholars critical of this stand include Richard Neustadt (2008) and Schilling (1961), who argue that political power is pulverized and dispersed in the national government. They claim that there is a sharp difference between constitutional and legislative powers attributed to the president and the real political process. Bureaus hold specialized knowledge, the power to set the agenda, and the power to implement. They must rely on the president, but the reverse also holds true. A variety of issues present themselves when dealing with foreign policy and defence: (i) financial aid; (ii) sanctions; (iii) agreements; and (iv) military interventions, among others. It is not reasonable to argue that a small group centred around the president can engage in all these issues. Furthermore, Congress 'holds the power of the purse'. In this sense, as previously stated, it is necessary to give special attention to the process of budgeting and acquisition, as it is the 'central arena' that provides the necessary resource mobilization and distribution to materialize any specific policy. Despite the president being an extremely important figure, it is not rational to assume that the individual occupying this role can dictate all of these outcomes. Budget is the material basis and a sine qua non condition for policy. This would be the basis of bureaucratic theory. Some bureaus, such as the military, are of notable importance. Huge budgets, real physical power, and close ties with other decision-makers make them especially influential.

An important breakthrough in this matter was the work of Herbert Simon on bounded rationality. Simon maintains that one person has a physical limitation when presented with the entire political agenda. The consequence is that an individual cannot possibly dedicate the necessary attention to optimizing all decisions (Simon, 1965). Due to natural cognitive functioning, decision-makers have limited information processing capabilities. Consequently, they do not objectively research all good information for the best outcome and must select the alternative that is acceptable or 'good enough'. Since responses in defence are not self-evident, theories of political process and decision-making have adopted Simon's theoretical advances.

Following Simon's breakthrough, incrementalism was presented to explain public policy. Changes in resource distribution and the political process do not usually differ radically from one year to the next. Decision-makers must process multiple agendas, and thus usually make choices aligned with the established status quo (Wildavsky, 1964). Explaining deviations from previous policy, especially in resource mobilization and distribution is thus the challenge assumed by some theories presented next alongside my criticisms and reasons for not adopting them for the development of the model.

It is not reasonable to argue that the formation of coalitions does not affect policy. They are the basis for constituency interest and representation. However, how they are formed and how they influence politics is another matter. Adherents of the first theory presented here, the ACF, attempted to engage in the matter (Sabatier, 2007). ACF maintains that coalitions are first formed at the micro-level, where diverse groups perceive a problem in a similar way and try to influence policy. Fundamental beliefs and general ontological assumptions about values and politics, which are a product of early socialization, make these issues salient and a source of cleavage. Beyond that, ACF holds that these beliefs, a product of informal networks of advocacy, are translated into specific policy issues within the coalition. In this second stage, the beliefs and issues, the environment, for example, pressure the formal political system by participation guidelines, rules, and budgetary applications of a program (Sabatier and Jenkins-Smith, 1993). The main criticism regarding ACF is its disregard for the relative influence of material interests and their place in beliefs. I do not deny the relevance of public mobilization as a part of the political process. Public opinion and self-interested individuals are a part of the process outlined by ACF – a senior player's stand will reflect constituency and pressure groups' interests. Motivation and core beliefs of a coalition are hard to assess and epistemologically unfruitful for explanation. I maintain that a focus on the source of human motivation to explain decision-making outcomes is unnecessary. The conflict among different stands reveals, by and large, what is being disputed and what affects the policy outcome.

The second theory addressed is the Punctuated-Equilibrium Theory. Relying on Simon's notion of bounded rationality and incrementalism of policy and budget, it attempts to explain drastic fluctuations in the distribution of resources and thus policy implementation. Incrementalism holds that policymaking is usually characterized by marginal changes and stability. For Punctuated-Equilibrium Theory, this holds true most of the time, although in specific cases political procedures produce large-scale departures from the past (True et al. 2007). When institutions, interests, and bounded rationality are set in motion, some issues 'catch fire'. Decision-makers' attention is drawn to the saliency and urgency of the issue. Punctuations are evident and most easily observed in budgeting, since budget translates into the result of conflicting interests. The theory holds that sufficient popular and group pressure or drastic events cause decision-makers to depart from incremental budget. Although I support the basic assumption that sufficient pressure influences decision-makers and agree that a wide range of variables motivate senior players, simplifying the analysis requires the supposition that senior players are self-interested and makes investigation and explaining more coherent with the materialist basis put forward in this Element. Budgetary punctuations can be observed in defence when the innovative material basis needs of senior players and external threat are present.

The third and final theoretical construction presented in this section is the one developed by Tsebelis regarding veto players. Change, new political outcomes, or, in the case of this Element, large-scale defence projects are departures from the prevailing regular policy. To depart from previous arrangements, Tsebelis maintains that agreement between veto players is required. This is precisely his definition of veto players (Tsebelis, 2005). According to the author, if preferences of veto players are close to the *status quo*, only incremental changes are possible. Now, if there is a need to form a consensus among different positions, significant changes are possible. Important to the theory developed here is Tsebelis' argument about the number of veto players.

Tsebelis contends that in a system with many veto players, as in the United States, bureaucracies and the judiciary will be more independent. However, the author argues that their role depends on whether or not there is consensus among the veto players; their independence varies in inverse proportion to such consensus. With fewer veto players, decisions become centralized. That is the case with countries like Brazil, for example both Congress and other supposedly auditing and societal players have a diminished role in defence decisions. Tsebelis theory is a general model which attempts to explain the role of veto players (Tsebelis, 2005). However, specific policymaking and the conflicting interests among bureaucracies and other players is not the aim of his theory. Although important inferences can be drawn from Tsebelis' framework, more in-depth explanations of the political process must be considered to assess large-scale defence projects. It is important, however, to emphasize that all three theoretical perspectives argue that a degree of consensus is necessary for implementation of policy, especially when it produces major changes.

2.3.2 Bureaucracies and Pulling and Hauling

So far, I have identified some main theories which engage in structure, actors, processes, and issues. These theories diverge in their epistemological/onto-logical propositions and consequently in their analysis of policy, including defence and decisions that might affect innovation. Despite their differences, these theories concur in the sense that there must be a minimum level of consensus to implement decision-making. The theories and processes studied in this topic can be applied to a variety of issues, extending the explanatory model. The assertion also holds true for threat and technological advancement, if economic development and systemic pressure, for example, are considered. However, legislation, actors' attributions, and the quality of issues are idiosyn-cratic. These factors limit the model since it must be adapted when analysing different policy outcomes. Despite such limitations, I argue that the possibilities for applying the model depend on simple propositions regarding the choice of actors, the relationship among them, scarce resource distribution, and the possible outcomes.

I now present what I consider one of the most elaborate theoretical constructions regarding internal politics, especially since it successfully opposes the more trad-itionalist self-adjusting and utility maximizing approach regarding state behaviour in the face of external constraints. This theory was advanced by Allison (1969) and Allison and Halperin (1972), with the intention of developing statements, assump-tions, concepts, and suggestive propositions. Bureaucratic theory was developed by Graham Allison to question Model I and propose two other models of decision-making in government. The paradigm enhances the understanding of intergovern-mental politics, by assessing, for example, Standard Operation Procedures (SOP's). Bureaucratic politics, in their words, 'an analytic paradigm', posed a difficult challenge for the proponents of Model I.[7] Furthermore, since the purpose here is

---

[7] Model II will not be addressed in detail here. It focuses mainly on SOPs, Bounded Rationality, Incrementalism and Organizational Procedures.

to address hypotheses from a domestic political angle, I claim that the BP model proposes a series of propositions and concepts that generate important research issues concerning the main theme explored in this Element.

Allison and Halperin's critique start from categorizing the self-adjusting and maximizing behaviour model of the state. What Allison calls the Rational Policy Model (Model I) consists of, in policy terms, an optimal decision made by a monolithic actor (the state) which selects from a formerly known range of options and chooses those which would maximize their strategic goals and objectives. The Rational Policy Model presupposes a cost and benefit analysis, analogous with the neoclassical theory of choice. This paradigm of analysis Allison calls Model I (Allison, 1969, pp. 692–695). The author proposes two alternative models: Modell II (the organizational model) and Model III (the bureaucratic model). These models are further addressed next. To test the theoretical development (models II and III) with empirical evidence, Allison makes a pertinent choice, applying Model I in a 'least probable case', the Cuban Missile Crisis, since it was 'a crisis decision, by a small group of men in the context of ultimate threat and thus this is a case of rational policy model par excellence' (Allison, 1969, p. 691). In his theory, Allison demonstrates that even in extremely urgent circumstances and with a small group responsible for developing a response, bureaucratic interests not only influence but also prevail.

Allison's critique of the Model I is that while attempting to explain a great number of situations and occurrences, the framework must deal with an enormous amount of information. Consequently, the model tends to make ad hoc explanations to explain foreign policy outcomes. When the model fails, authors who adhere to it invoke the notion of 'mistake' to explain suboptimal decision-making. Allison and Halperin (1972, p. 707) argue that the 'leaders who sit on top of organizations are not a monolithic group'. On the contrary, government is composed of organizations and individuals that compete and bargain through different channels. The authors hold that 'the government decisions are made not by rational choice but by the pulling and hauling that is politics (. . .) the apparatus of each government constitutes a complex arena for intra-national game' (Allison and Halperin, 1972, p. 707).

Pulling and hauling in politics eventually leads to a policy outcome. However, in accordance with the theory, the result is often a triumph of one group over others. What is more important, however, is that the result of such a political process tends to be suboptimal. In other words, it is different from what Model I would predict. If a minimum consensus must be achieved, some groups and interests will have to give in to more powerful ones. I argue that this relates firmly with Simon's bounded rationality since the information handed to the president passes through a significant number of large bureaucratic organizations (e.g., CIA and military), filtered by their own interests and political and economic aspirations. To assume otherwise would be unrealistic.

Allison's Model II tackles precisely this issue. Organizations usually operate through SOPS (standard operational procedures) which government leaders can disturb but not substantially control since these organizations have different parochial priorities, perceptions, and issues. Government, for the authors, is a large conglomerate of organizations and political actors whose stands differ sharply from what the government should do in a variety of issues. These actors are in constant competition and attempt to affect government decisions, actions, and, ultimately, policy outcomes.

An important distinction must be made in order to advance the topic. Allison and Halperin's theoretical construction propose concentric circles of decision-making, which ultimately distort the rationality presumption. Model III highlights the most relevant actors – senior players of national security policy – major political figures, the heads of major national security organizations, including intelligence, the military (. . .), the organization that manages budgetary allocations, and the economy (Allison and Halperin, 1972, p. 47). Around senior players, a circle of the so-called junior players is formed. These actors can be at lower levels of hierarchy but, nonetheless, affect the results of policy. It is easy to imagine a middle-level bureaucrat choosing to do things differently. In military engagement, such distortions of decision can have important consequences.

As this study investigates large-scale defence projects, it is essential to trace the senior players in the respective arena, since 'the mix of players will vary depending on the issue and type of game' (Allison and Halperin, 1972, p. 47). In the bureaucratic dispute, it is also necessary to note the moves of those players in opposition to the project. 'Those who opposed the decision, or who oppose the action, will manoeuvre to delay implementation, to limit implementation to the letter but not the spirit, or even to have the decision disobeyed' (Allison and Halperin, 1972, p. 53). In large-scale defence projects, delays and budget or organizational limitations can be crucial for their success or failure.

Even though bureaucratic theory is applied in various contexts, and as such has been a target of criticism, simple propositions can be inferred from the theory which can sustain a precise analysis. The most relevant contribution from bureaucratic theory I considered for this Element is that organizations usually seek to maximize their budget and prestige and protect their parochial task, for example, flying in the Air Force. Furthermore, SOPs usually result in inertia, dramatic changes occur during periods of budgetary feast, periods of prolonged budgetary famine or performance failures (Allison, 1969, p. 701).

The US Appropriation and Authorization Committees in Congress and the floor voting aftermath are inevitably *senior players* since they can alter the proposed presidential budget. The floor voting results depend on their appraisal of the political status quo. Congressional Budget Office, GAO, and the CRS provide decision-makers with valuable information regarding the fundamental traits and budgetary prospects of the project. Within the Executive, regarding defence, the military holds extraordinary power. However, the different forces will dispute regarding preferences. Each organization will privilege their own projects. The OSD and its leading officials are decisive to the project's future. Within the military, priorities are decided within the Joint Chief of Staff and the COCOMS. Alongside the president and the Secretary of Defence, these are considered senior players.

In some countries, Brazil, for example, the disputes occur mainly within the military, as Congress and auditing agencies have a diminished role. Decisions are usually made by the military in partnership with the private sector, when beneficial to the former. The Executive, especially in the years of civilian ministers, also have influence, albeit constrained by the power of the military. This represents a democratic deficit within the decision-making structure of the country's defence policy and may be seriously detrimental to the success of large-scale projects. The Armed Forces lack civilian oversight in budget, doctrine, and organization. This is a historical situation in Brazil, which has gone through military *coups*.

2.3.3 BP Criticisms and Theoretical Premises

Bureaucratic theory is the idea that decision-making is dispersed within nation government and the disputes among contending groups will define decisions. When bureaucratic theory was first developed, it was a target of harsh criticisms (Krasner, 1972; Freedman, 1976). I will put forward my own criticisms of the theory, in order to maintain coherence with the general model proposed here. Despite a critical view of some aspects of the theory, Allison and Halperin offer a framework that significantly influences the premises adopted here.

Although perception and values are in no way denied as a source of decision-making in this Element, the objective of this study is to investigate an empirical phenomenon that goes beyond a mere analysis, and thus, it is necessary to draw a *ceteris paribus* on these variables, as done with external threat. Bureaucratic politics provides a powerful paradigm for the analysis of decision-making, but there are some elementary issues to be outlined. 'Shared values and perceptions', 'self-interested individuals', and 'the stand of a player depends on his seat' are not necessarily contradictory (Allison and Halperin, 1972). However, they are difficult to combine into an analytical framework, in the sense of applying methodologies drawn from a conceptual framework towards operationalizing analysis in real-life situations. The richness of process description can limit focused studies to excessively historical, idiosyncratic accounts. Developments which further include these variables have proved themselves not applicable to the complexity of political process, except in very specific cases (Rosati, 1981; Welch, 1998). To shield themselves from criticisms, these scholars added a range of variables, partly compromising a powerful and insightful model of analysis: 'Each player's probability of success depends upon at least three elements: bargaining advantages, skill and will in using bargaining advantages, and other players' perceptions of the first two ingredients' (Allison and Halperin, 1972, pp. 53–54). Although the importance of stakeholders' personal traits is not denied, it is held here that it is unfruitful for analysis to attempt to trace these aspects, since the complexity and individuality of the subject is hard to access and trace. In this case, outcome is more important than the source.

The framework developed by Allison and Halperin (1972) is, however, a source of valuable propositions for the study of defence policy. The authors offer insights that are endorsed in this Element. Decisions reflect considerable compromise and are rarely tailored to facilitate monitoring. Therefore, senior players have great difficulty in checking on faithful implementation of a decision. As stated, I adhere here to the premise that organizations engage in pulling and hauling, attempting to maximize budget, prestige, and their parochial task. I also adhere here, in line with the previously mentioned premise, to the idea that we can reasonably expect that for the most part, a player will maximize his own interests.

The theories revised in this section share characteristics: none of them deny the need for a minimum level of consensus to implement policy, be that the mobilization around a salient issue, coalitions interested in policy change, or dispersed veto players. Presidents occupy a privileged position and are unique actors, a fact never denied by BP researchers. Nonetheless, presidents have to offer in order to achieve, they depend on a complex and vast network of decision-makers, among them, veto players (Tsebelis, 2005). Some theories rely specifically on individual human traits. However, is it possible to precisely infer intentions or beliefs relying solely on speeches, decisions, or actions? Personality traits, apart from having to rely on profound psychological and neurological tracing techniques, are also and further circumscribed by historical particularities. Core beliefs, informal networks, and so on lack a precise model for theory building. Besides from being hard to operationalize in empirical work, there is no guarantee that the researcher is dealing with true core beliefs, which will result in policy outcomes. Beliefs are hard to measure or even describe. Furthermore, they tend to be hard to assess.

2.3.4 Data and Hypothesis

I have argued that players are guided by enhancing their material interests and position, which are related to their stand in the government. Senior players vary according to the issue since, for example, different departments or congressional committees are divided by subject. Nevertheless, senior players are traceable, conflicting objectives can be observed, and the outcome derives from the possibilities created by this scenario. Materiality and thus budget disputes are at the core of most issues.

Given the premises already outlined, it is possible to infer that senior players' stands already incorporate other variables that the literature considers important without contradicting the assumption that they are in general guided by self-interested material and positional goals. I maintain then that public opinion, electoral concerns, constituency, and interest groups are already reflected and do not contradict a senior player's self-interested stand. Given that, the independent variable inferred here is that:

> The success of a large-scale project, defined as accomplishment of the project's initial purposes (with the SC outlined previously), is strongly influenced and positively related to the degree of consensus between and within Congress and the Executive. This hypothesis entails the need for three auxiliary hypotheses:
>
> a) The degree of consensus, nonetheless, depends on the Executive side: to reach an outcome of compromise between self-interested individuals and organizations within and among the services and within and among the OSD and the Office of Management and Budgeting (OMB). This entails the need for solid civil–military balance, which holds true for the relationship between Congress and the military.
>
> b) The Congressional role is crucial, and its internal scale of consensus depends on a compromise between self-interested individuals and organizations within and among the main committees of the issue (House and Senate Armed Services Committee (HASC/SASC), House and Senate Budget Committees (HBC/SBC), and the House and Senate Appropriation Committees (HAC/SAC)). Furthermore, there is a need for consensus building on the floor to approve the bills and guidelines issued by the committee.
>
> c) The split between the Senate and the House on this matter must be negotiated.

On Capitol Hill and in the White House, the high success of a large-scale defence project is understood here as a scenario where production reaches full development and scale production in accordance with its initial objectives. Failure is understood here as a low achievement in comparison with the project's initial goals and SC, and ultimately the cancelation of the project.

This correlates with the amount Congress grants in terms of resources to the project, which is a function of their need and the project's advancements in terms of technological feasibility and operational capacity through the project's lifecycle. The difference between the amount requested and granted by Congress is an important indicator of the project's success or failure prospects. It is necessary to highlight that this effort might be diminished by the focus on comparative parameters and not a deep *process-tracing* investigation of each project. Nonetheless, according to the stand taken by senior players and the amount granted to the project throughout its cycle, I attribute a score from low to high regarding the consensus built between and within Congress and the Executive. If main commissions, floor vote, and the Armed Forces are aligned with investing in the project, that is a high consensus scenario. Major opposition, doubts regarding feasibility, and disputes in the OSD are a clear sign of low consensus.

Although the analysis chosen here is mainly qualitative, strength of consensus requires some parameters of analytical guidance (Dall'Agnol, 2022). The reconstruction of some events can reveal (i) disagreements among senior players, attempts to use veto powers and harsh bargaining observed through the process, briefly outlined in the main hypothesis, and more detailed in the subsequent part, signify lower consensus. Since the main *senior players* are in a pulling and hauling scenario, which will not privilege the project's success, (ii) parochial interests, including inter-service rivalry, interferes negatively with a consensus building process; bureaucracies are known to the budget maximizers and prestige seekers, in this case, higher authorities or a consensus building within the Armed Forces is necessary for the project's prospects, (iii) major divisions between civil and military preferences, for example fiscal austerity versus budget expansion options, interfere in the dispute for consensus regarding the projects; especially in times of peace, fiscal austerity is privileged and the major projects might face cuts in their budgets, (iv) partisan opposition among senior players can dampen the strength of consensus required for the success of large-scale projects; commissions are formed by leadership from one party; however, budget is voted in the floor, which requires a bipartisan minimum level of consensus, and (v) the difference between the budget expectations and new challenges of the project from its beginning and during the process has a direct relation with consensus building; if all the actors involved are extremely dedicated to the project and faithful to its outcomes, chances are that it will present efficient and effective results, like the Manhattan project or the Nautilus Nuclear Propelled Submarine project.

In the next section, I turn to the comparative case analysis is to test the theoretical framework developed here. The cases were chosen in an attempt to vary the proposed parameters, including the international scenario, the budgetary disputes among forces and other political actors and the International System at the time of the project.

3 Large-Scale Defence Projects

This section is dedicated to testing the theoretical framework built with the proposed case studies. In epistemological terms, this Element endorses a middle-range theory.[8] This kind of construction lies in between nomothetic and idiographic forms of inquiry. Even so, there are methodological techniques that allow the researcher to identify solid causal connections. *Process-tracing* along with the Historical Comparative Method, as explained in the Introduction section, can identify the mechanisms present and absent in the same phenomenon and, thus, allow us to infer the causal relations. Process-tracing was conducted extensively in previous works (Dall'Agnol, 2022), in which the cases were more meticulously analysed, including, for instance, the submarine Nautilus. Here I address the principal parameters and arguments relating to the cases and main changes which accompanied their development, giving special emphasis to the marks I have chosen to characterize a project's lifecycle. My purpose is not to thoroughly examine the details of each project here.

This Element builds on previous works and attempts to refine the theoretical framework and especially to organize the data and arguments in a more rigorous and parsimonious way. I posit that the level of success based on the SC has a strong correlation with the independent variables. Beyond that, throughout the project's lifecycle, they have a high explanatory power regarding actors' responses to new events. The more a project reaches the advanced levels of its lifecycle, the more success criteria are met, and thus the more likely it is to succeed. It is the independent variables proposed and the systemic relation among them that makes the project advance, stagnate, or ultimately be cancelled. In order to demonstrate that, case of failure (FCS), moderate failure (B-2 Bomber), and moderate success (F-35) are now investigated. The choice of the cases refers to the methodological stand taken. The purpose is to isolate the variables which act in detriment or make a project successful. Highly innovative projects were analysed to explain innovation. There was an attempt to vary the Military Services. The Marines are contemplated by the F-35, but the Navy was left out. I analysed the Navy's Propelled Submarine Nautilus in other studies (Dall'Agnol, 2022), although to the lack of data I opted to leave it out of this Element.

---

[8] A middle-range theory does not have the ambition of classical positivism to generalize all its findings. The hypotheses confirmed are extended firstly to the phenomena investigated. Further generalization is definitely an objective, but not a necessary one.

In the following sections I will test the theoretical framework built so far in this Element. I will trace the action of *senior players* and their stands regarding the projects and the budgetary amount awarded to each case. I will test if technical feasibility is a sine qua non condition and, furthermore, if, as time passes, stakeholders tend to lose faith in the project if it does not demonstrate technological advancements. External threat is a key element to test since the projects vary from the early 1980s, where threat was high, to the 1990s, where threat was low, to the 2020s, where threat is definitely building up. Stakeholders will respond to threat by awarding resources to the projects.

3.1 The Future Combat Systems

I start the comparative case analysis with a failed project to highlight the absence of the phenomenon which enables a project to reach the advanced stages of its lifecycle as an efficient and effective weapon system. In this sense, negative cases are important to infer causality and to demonstrate the explanatory potential of the proposed variables. The FCS is considered here a complete failure since none of the SC proposed are met. As highlighted in the Introduction section, the SC are both effectiveness and efficiency measures. Efficiency refers to time, cost, and performance, while effectiveness refers to stakeholder's need and operational success. In defence, I argue that efficiency is subordinate to effectiveness.

I analyse the FCS and the reasons for its failure. The project was cancelled before reaching procurement, not delivering its components and having sunken R&D costs. In the FCS, consensus and political support faded as the project failed to deliver results. As the program advanced in procurement, the extremely immature technologies did not provide decision-makers with the confidence needed to grant the Army resources for the program. Despite the Army's best efforts at engaging Congress, constant cost and schedule uncertainties and delays made the FCS a target of scrutiny and criticism. The external environment changed, and the FCS could not deliver the necessary capabilities to counter the threats in Iraq and Afghanistan. The FCS was conceived within a doctrinal concept, which had emerged with vigour in the US Army by the mid-1990s. The Army developed, alongside the Defense Advanced Research Project Agency (DARPA), consistent with the Revolution in Military Affairs (RMA) and the transformation in information technologies, the concept of Force XXI to modernize and prepare its doctrinal and technological features for future threats. The FCS, together with reorganization of modular deployable forces, was a family of technologies aimed to equip a whole brigade and provide situational awareness and the use of advanced information and communication technology. The key aspect of the FCS was to transform the Army into an integrated, rapidly deployable, and flexible quick responsive front.

Regarding doctrinal concepts, the main idea was to reorganize the Army into smaller, self-sufficient, and interchangeable Brigade Combat Units of 4,000 soldiers. The goal was to deploy forces globally at a rate of 96 hours for a combat unit, 120 hours per division, and thirty days for five divisions (Pernin et al., 2012). This would make the FCS Brigade Combat Team (BCT) 60 per cent more rapidly deployable than the heavy Brigade Combat Teams. The purpose was to outmanoeuvre and surprise enemy forces. This would mean challenges in technological innovation, procurement, and threat response.

The idea of a fast, modular, and deployable force was conceived alongside the development of twenty-three weapon systems. These included more fuel-efficient vehicles, lighter armour, lighter armoured vehicles, and vertical take-off and landing (VTOL) aircraft and sensors. The VTOLs were an essential part of the 'air mechanized' concept, which consists of rapidly manoeuvring Army units. Armoured vehicles and personnel and associated logistics would be moved into the operational area. This family of technologies had the purpose of providing the units with access to the situation and engaging enemy forces with precision and speed before they could direct fire from an ambush position. The centrepiece of the FCS was the network. It would integrate all components keying advanced sensors, gathering information and data from multiple sources, and feeding the vehicles. This would create situational awareness. The sensor and communication technologies spread across the UAVs and the ground vehicles would enhance logistic readiness. This combination of doctrinal innovations and the family of technologies associated with them would represent the Army's future.

The FCS was conceptualized based on the Army's vision of future threats and their perspective for the need of radical modernization, both technological and doctrinal. The main idea was to build a network of interconnected systems to create situational awareness and rapid deployment of the troops. This would rely on light armour and vehicles, on information technology, unmanned aerial vehicles (UAVs), and precise ammunition. They would be integrated by a digital network to provide all the systems with instant information and coordination. In its concept, heavy armour would not be needed since the enemy would be engaged without time for a rapid heavy response. The problem is that the technologies were largely immature and unreliable, and this would erode confidence in the project as other interests and necessities were pressuring decision-makers.

The FCS was ambitious, not only in its technological development goals. It was inspired in the Army After Next (AAN)/Objective Force games conducted in the 1990s. Although the FCS was envisioned to prepare for all future threats, they were grounded on the assumption that future conflicts would involve major conventional ground combats between nations. These major regional conflict operations, as they became known within the DoD, were the foundation of the concepts which inspired the FCS, although its proponents advocated for the advantages that the FCS would bring to the Army to fight irregular warfare. The FCS was largely conceived to prepare for large cross-border invasions. This would largely influence the budgeting and acquisition process over the years, since the United States' immediate threats were the wars in the Middle East, and, consequently, resources were prioritized to this end. According to Pernin et al. (2012, p. 14): 'Proponents of these concepts claimed that sensor and processor technology was becoming so advanced that in the next few years the 'fog of war' in the complex ground combat environment would largely be lifted, even at the lower tactical levels.' The fog of technological feasibility, acquisition, and oversight requirements and political support, however, were a totally different matter.

The technological development was grounded in the concept of evolutionary acquisition and spiral development.[9] This would be another source of political turmoil since this kind of acquisition strategy was conceived to further increment mature and deployable technology and that was not the case with the FCS. Furthermore, the program was already singular in the sense that it was not a conventional acquisition process of a weapon system, but multiple weapon systems that would deliver results in the operational theatre conjointly. The lack of technological feasibility, the imminent in-theatre costs of the war, and the subsequent political pressure would seriously damage the efforts of the proponents of the FCS.

General Shinseki, one of the projects' first proponents, and Army Chief of Staff (1999–2003), set the goal for the project to be delivered by 2010. Cost and schedule volatility would, however, be a serious problem. A Concept and Technology Demonstration phase was divided into two parts. In February 2000, competition started between four industry teams and the contract was signed between DARPA, Boeing, and SAIC, which was to be referred to as the Lead Systems Integrator (LSI).[10] This form of contract, as it transferred to Boeing much of the Army's usual responsibilities, was to be a target of criticism. In this case, the government most likely was at an informational disadvantage, with adverse selection and moral hazard.

---

[9] Evolutionary acquisition and spiral development were formally incorporated in DoDs acquisition strategy in 2000, in Directive 5000.1 and its revised version of 2003, alongside with Directive 5000.2. It consists of deploying initial capabilities of a weapon system and receiving quick feedback from the end users, so that the technologies can be incremented and further developed while being tested.

[10] An LSI is an enhanced prime contractor. The LSI subcontracts works with other firms and participates in decisions regarding program management and collaborates in functions usually conducted solely by defence acquisition officials. Hence, this form of contract gives the LSI a large autonomy in conducting the program.

In its first years, despite the program having many problems, Congress remained supportive and granted the Army the amount requested of budget authority between fiscal years 2002 and 2004. However, the FCS was to be a case of acquisition turmoil, subject to constant scrutiny and dispute and budgetary volatility. Despite the Army's best effort, support in the Hill, auditing agencies and even inside the OSD was not achieved. Furthermore, the immature technologies and the ongoing wars in Iraq and Afghanistan pressured the decision-makers to prioritize other programs, as the FCS failed to correspond to their needs.

The program entered Milestone B in 2003. In accordance with US Code § 2432, the program managers prepare and submit to Congress an annual Selected Acquisition Report (SAR). The SAR provides cost, schedule, performance, and program unit costs data and projections. At Milestone B, the FCS program was estimated at $77 billion (2003 dollars). In all, $18 billion would be directed to R&DT&E (research, development, testing, and experimentation), $59.1 billion to procurement, and $600 million (2003 dollars) to military construction. The unit cost was the brigade and was estimated at $5.2 billion. Total lifecycle costs of the program, including personnel, O&M, and others, were estimated at $149 billion at Milestone B. The schedule for delivering Full Operational Capability could be met by delivering one fully equipped brigade and the Army proposed to deliver it in December 2012, followed by the Full-Rate Production decision in June 2013. The Army planned on producing the fourteen remaining brigades at a rate of one per year in 2009 and 2010 and two per year until 2017 (Pernin et al., 2012).

Throughout FCS's development, however, the Army's estimates were constantly challenged by auditing agencies and specialists. The FY 2004 National Defence Appropriation Act (NDAA) required auditing reports and greater detail in the FCS budget justification of the materials submitted. The House Acquisition Committee argued that the Army had to substantially improve justification for the various components of the program to compete for resources. The program had to be restructured as soon as 2005. The new baseline was set in November and changed the FCS program cost projections from $78 billion to $120.2 billion. The unit cost (brigade) climbed to approximately $6 billion.

After restructuring of the program, Congress hardened its demands. In the years up to the program's formal cancelation in 2009, the legislators would not grant the program the amount requested by the Army. The lack of confidence by the decision-makers in the program led to more oversight and scrutiny, which led to more cuts. Cost reviews and budgetary volatility were a sign of the Army's lack of support for the program at the Hill. Congressional committees did not grant the Army the amount they requested (Figure 6), and as the project's lifecycle went on, more cuts and scrutiny came from Congress, despite the Army's intensive lobbying. Congressional committees did not grant the Army

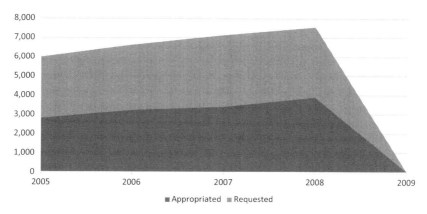

Figure 5 Requested versus appropriated amount for the FCS (current dollars)
Source: DoD Comptroller, 2023. The author.

the amount they requested (Figure 5), and as the project's lifecycle went on, more cuts and scrutiny came from Congress, despite the Army's intensive lobbying.

The FY 2005 NDDA required independent analysis of the program costs and technological feasibility to be submitted to Congress and demanded that the Secretary of the Army establish and implement a detailed FCS program strategy. The CBO reported, in February 2005, that the full costs of the program were still unknown since the program was still in the early stages of development. In this report, the CBO recommended the cancellation of the program except for R&D to explore promising technologies for future use or the delay of the FCS fielding from 2011 to 2015. The GAO issued an analysis in the same year, which stated that the program was not appropriately applying efforts to mature its critical technologies. The agency argued that the technologies were too immature, and this increased the risk of schedule delay and cost growth. Congress became sceptical of the program and recommended cuts to the Army's FCS budget.

The Army increasingly advocated for the FCS's budget maximizing and disregarded dissenting positions. There was a lack of competing conceptual ideas. The program was apportioned through forty-one states and the Army made its best effort to engage with Congress. Nonetheless, Congress did not defend the funding request for long. As cost estimates were constantly being questioned and changed, core technological systems were far from being demonstrated and schedule delays became constant, concurring important programs challenged the FCS. The immediate needs of the stakeholders pressured resource distribution to other programs since the FCS was failing to demonstrate its feasibility and urgency.

When the HAC and the SAC reduced funding for the FCS, the Army reacted by lobbying intensely. Nevertheless, no matter how much the Army discussed with members of the Congress, they could not convincingly demonstrate the return of billions of dollars appropriated for research and development nor could they provide the legislators with a consistent narrative in defence of the program. Important voices in Congress, such as Senator John McCain, member of the SASC (Senate Committee on Armed Services), became vocal and criticized several aspects of the program, including oversight difficulties, management problems, climbing costs, and uncertain priorities. The OSD began responding to congressional reticence to fund the FCS. At this point, the support for the FCS began to erode within the Executive.

Cost estimates by the GAO and the CAIG (Cost Analysis Improvement Group) were far higher than those made by the Army. The CAIG projected $300 billion (2003 dollars) for the program's total lifecycle, and the GAO estimated the total cost of the program to be $160.7 billion, 73% higher than the Army's initial estimate (Pernin et al., 2012). Immature technology would diminish confidence in the program and in its cost estimates. Bureaucratic disputes for budget grow in this uncertain scenario since decision-makers must prioritize in order to allocate resources. Navy shipbuilding and missile defence, for example, were constantly being seen as important, thus threatening FCS's budget. Consequently, resource decrements increased in FY 2006 and 2007.

Evolutionary acquisition, the chosen development strategy for the FCS, was not well suited for the program. The technology was not mature enough for deployment to generate feedback and further development. For this kind of technological development strategy, it is crucial that technological feasibility must have sound readiness in the case of ongoing military engagement. The feedback from the end user, in this case the soldier, must be based on a system that is at least functional in battle. According to Ellman (2009, p. 16): 'The initial increment is supposed to be functional and survivable in its own right.' In the case of the FCS, technological feasibility was low and did not mature enough. As early as 2005, GAO identified that (2005, p. 301)

> [t]here is not enough knowledge to say whether the FCS is doable, much less doable within a predictable frame of time and money. Yet making confident predictions is a reasonable standard for a major acquisition program given the resource commitments and opportunity costs they entail. Against this standard, the FCS is not yet a good fit as an acquisition program.

The constant schedule and cost reviews indicate that the program had problems in its technological development and in its lack of political support. The relation between technological feasibility and political support is systemic and they are both necessary for a successful innovative project. In the case of the FCS, as the data and documents demonstrate, both were lacking. By 2009, support in Congress and the Executive had withered completely.

During the years of the FCS, both the relative distribution of material capabilities and the direct threat changed in disfavour of the United States. However, besides not meeting the necessary conditions for success, the FCS was not suited to the ongoing threats. The counterinsurgency missions the Army was performing in Iraq and Afghanistan showed that the fog of war was not lifted by technology. The difficult environment and the tactics used by the enemy would surprise the US soldiers and make technological asymmetry less important. Immature technologies posed a danger, and other budgetary demands became increasingly urgent. As argued by Kaeser (2009, p. 2): 'These cost burdens go far beyond the FCS. They interact with other procurement programs, current warfighting needs, the cost to compensate for past wartime wear and losses, and the expansion of its manpower strength.'

The cutting-edge technology, immature and costly, was not responsive to external threat. As stated, the program was conceived to engage with powerful state actors or unstable nuclear states, such as Iran and North Korea. Large conventional armies such as China or Russia could justify the FCS, as the United States would use its technological advantage to explore asymmetric weaknesses or gaps. Since it was conceived for large-scale conventional engagement, decision-makers did not perceive the FCS as suited for the necessities of the time. Secretary of Defense Robert Gates stated that the lower weight, fuel efficiency, and informational awareness, which were expected to compensate for less armour, did not reflect the lessons of counterinsurgency and close quarters combat in Iraq and Afghanistan.

The Army did not have a clear grasp of which technologies were necessary and feasible. The FCS failed to respond to the ongoing external threat and the Army could not build a consensus in the political arena for the program. The FCS failed to demonstrate technological feasibility and to deliver appropriate estimates regarding cost, performance, and schedule. The program was formally cancelled on 23 June 2009. Table 1 clearly demonstrates the failure of the project both in efficiency and effectiveness parameters.

According to Todd Harrison, budget expert of the Center for Strategic and International Studies (CSIS): 'the FCS program was such a massive failure and a missed opportunity for Army modernization' (*apud* SPRENGER, 2016, p. 1). Other authors agree and point to the problems: 'The all-encompassing program was remarkable because there was no mechanism in place to periodically re-evaluate key assumptions, leading officials to charge forward without asking important

Table 1 FCS projections and results

Initial objectives	Results
Cost projection: $77 billion (2000 dollars)	Sunken $15 billion (current)
Schedule: 2017	Cancelled
Performance: Rapid deployment avoiding defence	Surprised by asymmetric warfare
Operational success: Engage in large conventional conflicts and with regional powers	Surprised by asymmetric warfare
Stakeholder's need: Modernize the Army	Focused on the ongoing wars

Source: The Author. US Comptroller Office.

questions along the way' Sprenger (2016, p. 1); or, as stated by Daniel Gouré (2011, p. 1), 'the security environment had changed and the FCS program had failed to deliver on its promise'. The formal cancellation came on 23 June 2009.

By the end, the FCS had already spent around $15 billion in R&D. Some of the programs remained at the time; although they were managed as individual programs, most of them cancelled in the following years.

For example, the Non-Line-Sight Cannon, which was eventually cancelled later in 2009. The Unattended Ground Sensors and the Class 1 Unmanned Air System, both reminiscent programs of the FCS, were cancelled in 2011 (Gouré, 2011, p. 1). The Manned Ground Vehicle was rearranged as the Ground Combat Vehicle, which was also cancelled in 2014 (Brockman, 2017). Consequently, '[a]lthough some of its components have been transferred to other programs, FCS is widely regarded as a failure, which has eroded confidence in Army acquisition capabilities from those both inside and outside the Army' (Pernin et al., 2012, p. 2). Therefore, the FCS lies firmly in the past.

In the case of the FCS's, Initial Operational Capability (IOC) was never reached, and thus its operational performance could not even be tested. Other interests and programs became priority, even though initially there was substantial support for the FCS. The Army became isolated in the defence of the program, which ultimately was cancelled without satisfying any parameter of success.

Whilst there is no precise measure to determine external threat, one can reasonably argue that crossroad tactics by radicalism do not pose a vital threat such as those that come from great power competition or even regional leaders. As such, threat level during the FCS can be regarded as low. Furthermore, even while countermeasuring the ongoing threat, the FCS failed: light armour and intelligence could not compensate for the losses, in this specific war scenario, of giving up heavy armour.

Despite the Army's constant effort at engaging with Congress, in the passing of FY's, FCS lost its support. Besides the project being innovative and promising investments in forty-one states, and its initial procurement support, politics is sensitive to uncertain cost and schedule projections. The DoD started to abandon the project as well. Concurrent pivotal projects and wartime costs began competing with the FCS. Decision-makers respond to constituencies, and the Army could not justify the resources needed for the FCS. Agencies such as the GAO and the CBO constantly criticized the program, and Congress demanded further oversight as the years passed. The amount appropriated for the project dropped and consensus was definitely not reached. The GAO and the CBO firmly asserted that technologies were extremely immature. Constant cost and schedule reviews, with disagreements among different auditing agencies and actors' referent to these metrics, demonstrated that technological development of the FCS was facing trouble. Some of the core technologies of the FCS were very far from demonstration, while others were only partially developed. Even if it was technologically feasible in the long term, what matters in procurement is the shorter term and the current needs of defence, especially when budgets are disputed. Political support started at a medium level and soon fell to low. Technological feasibility remained low during the lifecycle of the FCS. The systemic dynamics of innovation could not be met, and the program did not succeed in its ambitions.

3.2 The B-2 Stealth Bomber

The second case I examine, the B-2 stealth bomber, is considered on the failed spectrum regarding the SC delineated earlier. The B-2 was a highly ambitious program, which aimed at rendering the superior Soviet air defences with a long-range stealth bomber. It was conceived in a scenario of growing threat in the late 1970s and the beginning of the 1980s, which diminished drastically with the fall of the Soviet Union. The B-2 suffered constant schedule delays and cost overruns, which alongside the diminishing threat helped to fade its support from decision-makers, despite parochial interests. Technologically, it failed to demonstrate feasibility in time, and Clinton's bottom-up review cut its resources. Even so, twenty-one aircraft were procured and performed important conventional missions, and the program did meet some SC. It cannot be considered a complete failure, but the aircraft did not meet the criteria to be considered on the successful spectrum of large-scale defence projects.

By the late 1970s, United States' decision-makers were concerned with the eroding defence capabilities of the country, especially since the Soviet Union was growing its advantages regarding their radar systems, anticraft missiles, and fighter forces. There was a general perception among US officials that the country's strategic triad – land-based intercontinental missiles, long-range bombers, and submarine-launched missiles – was lagging behind and could become obsolete, especially regarding the manned bomber leg of the triad.

It was in this scenario of growing threat levels that the B-2 program was conceived.

In its conception, to counter Soviet defences, the B-2 program was initiated to build a long-range stealth bomber, to avoid detection, and thwart the enemy's capability of countermeasures. The idea was to hit the target and return without being detected. Stealth aircraft would have high assurance of penetration and would not have to fly at a breakneck speed, routes, or altitudes to avoid defence radars. The B-2 could be used alongside missiles for cross-targeting, to back-up assurance, or for the primary attack. While attacking fixed installations (political, economic, or military) or military forces (ships, aircraft, army vehicles, and personnel), the B-2 could open the area to future penetration by non-stealth aircraft. In theatre air operations, strategic stealth bombers would not be diverted from their primary missions to defend themselves since they would hardly be engaged by air defence. According to Welch (1989, p. 59): 'In air-to-air combat, surprise is an exceedingly strong factor. Even a small delay in detection can allow one aircraft to obtain a more favourable initial position that will provide dominance in the ensuing engagement.' The program was initially perceived as necessary by the decision-makers, and the advantages seemed promising. However, there were many technical and political obstacles for the program to succeed. Achieving a stealth aircraft, with many new design components necessary, would pose technological feasibility, cost, and schedule challenges.

Detection of an aircraft can be achieved through radar, infrared, visual sighting, acoustic, or electronic emission methods. Especially challenging was the Soviet's advanced long-range radar capability. Radars send pulses of electromagnetic energy that hit the target and bounce back to the transmitter. Electronic techniques can provide, through the receiver, information about a target aircraft's presence, speed, direction, and size. The infrared sensors identify a heat presence that looks different from the air around the supposed attacker. Acoustic sensors detect the noise coming from the aircraft. As for electronic sensors, the electromagnetic emissions radiated by the aircraft are identified.

The first challenge in developing a stealth aircraft was to reduce its RCS (radar cross section), the way a radar can identify it. To minimize its RCS, the

B-2s contractor, Northrop, conceptualized the blend between the wings into the fuselage, making the aircraft a 'flying wing', a very short and broad wing, with no tail. All-wing aircraft were not entirely new at the time, but they did impose challenges: 'they do not have an established aerodynamic track record at very low altitudes. Any aircraft based on an unproven design faces a long and potentially tumultuous fight testing program' (Brown, 1988, p. 355). The aircraft would have to rely on computer-controlled vectoring, which would involve major technological advances. The B-2 program would count on hiding the engine and its inlets buried in the body of the aircraft and blending the cockpit within rounded wing surfaces. Furthermore, stealth advances would have to come from the coating of the aircraft's skin with materials that absorb radar-reflectivity. Moreover, assigned to strategic missions, it would have to survive the blast from its own nuclear weapons. The right materials for this scenario would be a further challenge to the B-2's designers. Even though the growing threat level was concerning decision-makers, mundane material problems could disrupt the entire program.

The initial plan was to produce 132 B-2 bombers, at an estimated cost of $36.6 billion in 1981 dollars. Northrop Grumman was awarded the contract on 2 November 1981, with the plan to ramp up peak production to thirty aircraft per year, after the proposed test deadline of 1987. According to this schedule, the B-2 would reach initial operational capability by 1990. However, bureaucratic disputes and economic inefficiency would seriously dampen the effort of the program's proponents. According to Rebecca Grant (2012, p. 2): 'B-2's history was one marked by economic inefficiency, by bureaucratic politics and technological feasibility doubts, and economic calculations'. Stacy and Guzinger (1996, p. 29) argue that 'the B-2 program, in particular, demonstrates the enormous difficulty of making rational defence spending decisions purely on the basis of US national security interests'.

I claim here that diminishing threat level, lack of consensus among specialists and main actors, bureaucratic disputes, and technological feasibility challenges led to unsatisfactory results for the project. These problems were intertwined over the following decades and affected the ultimate results of the program. I argue that with lack of the necessary competitive pressure posed by external threat and since the program failed to deliver results in time, decision-makers did not perceive the program as feasible or urgent, and cut the resources for the program. Parochial interests are not sufficient to make a project successful since other interests and bureaucratic actors pressure the budget. In times of falling defence budgets, when a project faces cost and schedule overruns and technological doubts, decision-makers allocate resources to other programs.

Throughout its development, the B-2 was the target of much criticism and congressional scrutiny, since, among other things, it was a costly large-scale program, with tangible concurrent strategic alternatives. Much of the debate surrounding the B-2 took place in the late 1980s and early 1990s, in a drastically changing scenario, the end of the Cold War, which would put in doubt the program's strategic objectives and necessity. Specialists and key actors of decision-making debated the program at a time when there were drastic defence budget reductions, which presented concurrent programs and different interests as an ever-greater challenge. Disputes among those defending their constituencies, alongside priority debates and disputes within the Armed Forces, were intensified. Cost projections would be a serious matter since the original estimates were constantly being revised and different actors provided different figures. The technology was new and no more than estimates could be made at the time. Welch (1989) highlights that at the time, to a substantial degree, many of the costs of incorporating stealth were not known.

By the late 1980s many concurrent options were presented by specialists to the decision-makers, and serious doubts around the need for the B-2 arose. The next (after 1988) elected president would face an immense challenge, with cuts in defence budgets – something would have to give. Brown (1988, p. 351) argued that given this scenario, 'the fate of the B-2 would probably hinge on cost consideration and seemingly mundane procurement issues'. The author argued that if the deployment decision was made, it should focus exclusively on engineering development testing, to provide decision-makers with the necessary information to make an acute decision, with a solid cost-effectiveness evaluation. This would release budgetary resources in the near term for other pressing military needs.

Authors and specialized agencies, in the face of a weakening Soviet Union, questioned the strategic necessity for B-2s. Brown (1988, p. 353) stated that cruise missiles were already tested and reliable and were more effective than bombers since 'the smaller, single-engine cruise missile has much lower RCS and Infra-Red Signature (IRS) than a manned aircraft'. In accordance, Brower (1990) argued that Soviet defences had already been made largely obsolete by cruise missiles. Brown (1988) maintained that, strategically, there was no compelling case for the B-2. He stated that the B-1B would be effective as the bomber leg of the triad for twenty-five to forty years and cruise missiles such as the ALCMs (Air-Launched Cruise Missiles) and ACMs (Advanced Cruise Missile) already fulfilled the requirements for the B-2's purposes. Brower (1990) claimed that B-2s would not be effective against mobile targets since these hidden targets could be jammed, and the use of simple countermeasures, such as decoys, would significantly reduce the number of targets that the penetrating bomber could destroy. It was reported by some authors that the proponents of the project could not uphold the argument that the B-2 would be needed in the early 1990s and there was no rationale for an accelerated procurement program. As for conventional missions, Brown (1988) maintained, in accordance with several critiques, that the B-2 was too expensive and the Air Force already had recourse to the B-52, B-1B, FB-111 bombers and the F-17, F-15, and F-16 fighters to be used in these scenarios.

Technological feasibility issues were also a target of criticism. There were constant problems with aerodynamics and materials, and these were not a superficial matter since they could derail the entire procurement program. Brown (1988) highlighted delays in the B-2 first flight test, increased cost estimation, Northrop's downsizing in production, and Congressional reticence in accelerating the program. The author asserts that decision-makers should focus primarily on prototype testing: 'The prototype testing stage of the process is also vitally important because it confirms that the weapon works as advertised and it allows the engineers to finalize the design of the system before high-rate production begins. Building a prototype also helps to confirm cost and schedule estimates' (Brown, 1988, p. 357). Testing demonstrates technological feasibility and any delays can seriously affect the decision-makers' stand on the program. According to Brown (1988, p. 25): 'In fact, none of the advantages the air force claims for the B-2 can withstand careful scrutiny.' In the light of reduced defence budgets, BP and different stands in Congress, the defence acquisition community would have a difficult time in reaching a consensus that would support the program.

The diminishing external threat, pressure from Congress to drastically cut military spending, technical difficulties, and repeated delays impacted the Air Force's plans for the B-2 by 1990. On 26 April, Secretary of Defense Richard Cheney proposed a reduction in the purchase of B-2 stealth bombers. The initial plans for procuring 132 bombers at an estimated cost of $75 billion (1990 dollars) were modified, and the Pentagon proposed buying 75 bombers for $61.1 billion. Besides the reduction in quantity, unit cost estimates were climbing. The $815 million per plane in the Air Force's plan already represented an increase of $275 million in comparison with 1989. Furthermore, operation and support costs, including fuel, maintenance, spare parts, and personnel tanker aircraft, were estimated to cost another $20 billion over twenty-five years for a force of sixty active duty bombers (Brower, 1990, p. 28). Brower estimated that, adding these factors, the B-2 force would probably cost $103 billion to acquire, operate, and support. Brower (1990) demonstrates that the program's estimated cost grew 12 per cent in real terms between 1981 and 1986, and 20 per cent in real terms between 1986 and 1989. The CBO reported, in 1990, that possible cost increases were to be expected, since there were unknowns regarding the program. The GAO (1990) reported that the cost of B-2's avionics tripled between 1988 and 1989 and was two years behind schedule. Despite important opposition and exorbitant costs, the program still had strength and, by 1990, Congress had already approved the development of fifteen B-2s.

The B-2 was a large-scale project, and similar to the FCS, Northrop's production line was spread around the country, through 48 states and 383 congressional districts. Northrop contributed to key Congressman campaigns. Furthermore, job creation and economic boosting, especially in California, Texas, and Washington – which benefited disproportionally from B-2 contracts – gave the program special constituency strength and challenged those opposed to the program. 'Northrop had contracted with almost 8,000 suppliers in 48 states and distributed $14 billion in subcontractors' (Stacy and Gunzinger, 1996, p. 8). Defenders of the B-2 held key positions in the early 1990s. The military procurement subcommittee was chaired by Duncan Hunter of California and the Majority leader of Procurement subcommittee was J. C. Watts (Oklahoma). Air Force officials stated that the program represented 'revolutionary aerial warfare' and was needed to carry US strategic forces into the next century. Despite the best efforts of the program's proponents, the necessary degree of consensus in support of the program could not be achieved and this was quintessential to the administration's decision to cut the program to seventy-five units in 1990. There was much uncertainty regarding the actual costs and different procurement options, and congressional oversight strengthened.

The HASC questioned the estimates and procurement plans of the Air Force, arguing that, with falling defence budgets, annual funding for the program would drop, raising its overall unit cost. The CBO stated that the program could cost $1.95 billion per unit, based on a total buy of thirty-three planes at a rate of two per year. If the program was immediately cancelled, $45 billion would be saved, although this 'would leave a force of 16 bombers with price tags of $2 billion each (CBO, 1993)'. The Air Force's plan of 132 bombers had already failed and the debate centred around deciding how many planes could be cut, taking into consideration the unit cost. Scale saves money, since R&D costs, for example, are fixed. According to Healy (1990, p. 1), the 1990 Air Force plan could reach a peak funding close to $10 billion. This was an 'impossible proposition' according to Rep. Les Aspin (D-Wis), chairman of HASC, when he was presented with the Bush Administration's proposed production schedule for the B-2. Les Aspin would become Secretary of Defense in Bill Clinton's government. Senator Alan Cranston stated that the CBO report confirmed what he had said from the outset. He argued that the only way to stop wasting money on the B2 program was to 'kill it outright – not a slice at a time, but once and for all' (Healy, 1990, p. 1).

Support for the program started to erode inside the Executive. The Defence Department's former procurement chief, Robert Castello, who held the position of undersecretary of acquisitions, said, in 1989, that the B2 program should be killed because of 'exorbitant costs, sloppy quality control and poor management by the company building high-technology aircraft' (Moore, 1989). Castello argued that the development of the aircraft was at the early stages and the Air Force could not calculate its true costs. In accordance with Brower (1988) and Brown (1990), he argued that the military did not need the new bomber, 'since it already had extensive existing strategic arsenal of missiles, submarines and bombers' (Moore, 1989, p. 1). With the failure of the Air Force and the programs proponents to provide key decision-makers with a strong case in favour of the B-2, it was just a matter of time before the program was cancelled. Eventually, auditing agencies increased scrutiny and the program became a good target for expenditure cuts in Clinton's bottom-up review of the defence budget.

A CBO report in 1993 stated that 'the contractor has had difficulty in implementing changes to cost and schedule baselines needed to reflect changes to program schedules'. According to CBO (1993), the Air Force did 'not adequately describe cost estimates for B-2 development and procurement programs and does not specifically describe cost estimates for elements speci-fied by legislation'. The GAO (1995) released a study which reported that 'after 14 years of development and evolving mission requirements, including 6 years of flight testing, the Air Force has yet to demonstrate that the B-2 will meet some of its most important mission requirements'. The GAO highlighted that as for May 1995, the B-2 had completed only about 44 per cent of the flight test hours planned for meeting test objectives. The report concluded that '[a]fter 9 years of producing and assembling aircraft, Northrop Grumman, the prime contractor, continues to experience difficulties in delivering B-2s that can meet Air Force operational requirements. For the most part, aircraft have been delivered late and with significant deviations and waivers' (GAO, 1995). The program's failure in cost and schedule assessment and its delays in demonstrat-ing performance would further dampen the effort of its proponents. The demo-cratic Congress and the Bush administration eventually decided to cap procurement at twenty aircraft at a cost of $44 billion.

Bureaucratic politics certainly played a decisive role in the outcome of the B-2 project.[11] In the early 1980s, Ronald Reagan undertook a massive military build-up to pressure the Soviet economy and counter its growing capacities. The Air Force could make a compelling case for the penetrating bomber. As technological feasibility issues pressured the fate of the program alongside

---

[11] Jerry Stacy and Mark Guzinger (1996) developed a study investigating specifically the B-2 and bureaucratic politics in the mid 1990s.

cost and schedule overruns, and threat level diminished, decision-makers did not accept the Air Force's defence of the B-2. It is natural that a bureau, as stated earlier, tries to maximize budget and prestige, and protect its role. According to Halperin (1974, p. 28), 'the dominant view within the Air Force has been that its essence is the flying of combat airplanes designed for the delivery of nuclear weapons'. In taking stands on policy, budgetary, and strategic questions, thus, the Air Force has always 'sought to protect its role in the strategic delivery of weapons by air'. This does not resemble an instrumental rationality model of decision-making. However, the pulling and hauling between bureaucracies and decision-makers in the face of cutting budgets did not benefit the Air Force's plans for the B-2.

Eroding support for B-2 within Congress and the Executive peaked during Clinton's government. There was no consensual support or a strong majority in Congress of supporters of the B-2, which worked to the advantage of Clinton's administration and its objectives of cutting defence expenditures through its bottom-up review. With no imminent threat, decision-makers did not see the need for additional bombers. Within Clinton's government, OSD, led by Secretary Les Aspin, initiated a campaign to determine appropriate post–Cold War military strategy and force structure. There was a growing concern with fiscal matters within the government. In its program, the bomber force structure was limited, including twenty B-2 perceived as sufficient. With downsizing budgets, a major concern was conflict among services, since opening the door for more B-2s would result in requests from the services for new and expanded programs (Stacy and Guzinger, 1996). While Congress was put in a difficult position having to choose between additional B-2s and other procurement programs, such as the F-22, the president's decision prevailed and the 21[a] B-2 was the last to be procured. Decision-makers had agreed to halt the procurement of the B-2 bombers and the Clinton FY 1996 defence budget did not include money for additional bombers. The Air Force's plans had failed dramatically. Twenty-one planes were already operational and had been used for conventional missions. However, that was not the plan. Diminishing threat level, lack of consensus, and problems demonstrating technological feasibility led to cancellation at an astonishing unit level.

The actual real cost of the B-2 program had decreased from the original estimate of $36.6 billion (1981 dollars) to $29.07 billion (1981 dollars) by 1990. However, since the original estimate was based on the projection of 132 planes and the delivery was 21, the original estimate of unit cost was $277 million, which increased to a real unit cost of more than $1 billion (1981 dollars). By the mid-1990s, it had not proven its performance goals in relation to its main mission requirements and was still having trouble estimating costs and schedules (GAO, 1995; CBO, 1993). The first flight took place in 1989, and the first delivery in 1993. That represents a two-year delay in testing. Initial Operational Capability (IOC) was achieved in 1997, a seven-year delay according to initial projections. Although it entered IOC and was ultimately successful at testing, the decision to cancel had already been made. B-2 proponents could not sustain the overruns in cost and schedule and performance problems while convincing decision-makers of its importance.

The advances in technology during the process' effort were, however, substantial and unmatched by other air forces. The objective of the plane was adapted, and its chief role was changed to conventional weapons delivery, although still maintaining nuclear capability. The B-2 struck targets in Serbia in 1999, Afghanistan in 2001, and Iraq in 2003. The Air Force, however, continued to argue that despite the end of the Cold War, strategic warfare was vital and, furthermore, justified the bomber's central role since it was assigned to conventional missions. This is why the B-2 is rated on the failed spectrum. Despite delivery of twenty-one aircraft that had been operationally successful and technological advanced, the program was not efficient in terms of cost, schedule, and performance, and was not considered necessary by stakeholders and decision-makers. With no prospects for efficiency and effectiveness, decision-makers cancelled the project. What prevents it being considered a complete failure is that, ultimately, it proved itself worthy for engagement.

Technological feasibility issues were a constant problem, leading to frequent changes in cost and schedule projections. Bureaus had conflicting interests and the main actors involved could not reach a consensus. Congress commissions, the OSD, and specialists were not convinced of the expenditure and strategic necessities of the program. External threat, crucial to pressuring innovation, diminished drastically with the fall of the Soviet Union.

Technological feasibility was certainly another troubled issue. Large schedule and cost revisions reveal that the program faced constant technological challenges. Between totally unfeasible or totally feasible, there are degrees of technological challenges that impact decision-making and the success of the program. This can only be observed by the processing-tracing of the project's development. Over time, even though some of the proposed bombers were procured, the difficulties faced by development certainly discredited the project, raised doubts about its technological feasibility, and were a factor in its unsuccessful results. Technological feasibility grew from low to high. Even though it ultimately proved itself feasible, the uncertainties and challenges regarding its technical aspects worked against the proponents of the project.

With the diminishing threat and economic struggle faced by the Soviet Union at the end of the decade, the program was further challenged in terms of its necessity. Falling defence budgets, readjustment of the United States' priorities, and concurrent programs put the B-2 even more into question. The motivation of external threat for innovation and internal resources mobilization was not present. Finally, it is worth mentioning that external threat variation compelled the readjustment of the aircraft's purposes, changing its main objective from nuclear deterrence to conventional missions. Threat level fell to low during the years of the project.

While the Air Force, as expected according to BP theory, defended its assigned mission, monopoly of information and growing budgets, other players did concur. The fall of defence budgets led other services to bargain for their own priorities. And even within the Air Force, there were doubts and disagreements regarding prioritizing projects. Northrop defended the program and there were strong supporters of the B2 in Congress commissions, although not sufficient to build a consensus. Defenders of the B-2 were constantly questioned and summoned to hearings. The Pentagon was pressured to cut their plans for the B2. Clinton's administration and the OSD opposed the program in the context of the bottom-up defence review. Consensus was certainly not met, and this directly affected the final decision to procure only 21 B2 stealth bombers. With a total cost estimated around $45 billion, the B-2 is the most expensive individual aircraft ever made.

The unit cost of a B-2 was $2 billion by the twenty-first century. The project is not entirely a failure because it did develop important technologies and is used in conventional missions while still carrying strategic capacity. However, it neither satisfied stakeholders' needs nor efficiency criteria due to the factors I proposed in this Element: diminishing external threat, technological feasibility issues, and lack of consensus among *senior players*. Table 2 makes this clear.

Table 2 B-2 projections and results

Initial objectives	Results
Cost projection: $36.6 billion (1981 dollars)	$44 billion (1995 dollars)
Quantity projection: 132 units	20 units
Schedule: IOC by 1990	Achieved: IOC by 1997
Performance: Strengthen stealth Manned bomber penetration	Accomplished
Operational success: Engaging in Soviet's airspace, successfully engaging targets	Conventional missions
Stakeholder's need: Penetrate soviet's air defences	Technological advancements in stealth material

Source: The Author. US Comptroller Office.

According to the Augustin Laws, in the year 2054, the entire defence budget will purchase just one aircraft. This aircraft will have to be shared by the Air Force and Navy 3–1/2 days each per week except for leap year, when it will be made available to the Marines for the extra day.

3.3 The F-35

The F-35 is an ongoing program. However, its maturity alongside its long lifecycle permits a solid investigation for the purposes of this Element. A final assessment regarding its definitive status as successful or a failure is not possible. Nonetheless, the results of the project so far and its relationship with the independent variables employed here allow the inference of causality and the verification of the hypotheses proposed. The multirole fighter is placed on the successful spectrum of large-scale defence projects, consistent with the proposed model of analysis.

The F-35 was conceptualized as a fifth-generation aircraft to substitute an aging fleet and to integrate ongoing projects to develop a joint project for the Marines, Navy, and Air Force. Its objectives were both economic and military. It was to be cost-effective since it would replace separate fighter programs for these forces. Furthermore, the challenges of the International System required an innovative effort from the United States to maintain its air superiority edge. The new fighter would satisfy needs in common for all services, by providing variants to these services with increasing commonalities, supposedly reducing the costs of separate development programs. These were to include a Conventional Take-Off and Landing (CTOL) – the F-35A – for the Air Force, in order to replace the F-15, F-16, and the A-10 aircraft; a Short Take-Off and Vertical Landing (STVOL) – the F-35B – for the Marine Corps, to replace the CTOL F/A-18 and AV-88 strike fighters; and a carrier suitable fighter – F-35 C – for the Navy, to replace the F/A-18E/F. It would become a stealthy, data gathering and effective airplane, providing situational awareness and tactical superiority. There were, however, many challenges regarding cost and schedule overruns, which is the primary reason for its incomplete success. Nevertheless, the F-35 eventually proved itself technologically feasible, maintained political support, and became more necessary as threat level rose.

In its conception, the JSF integrated ongoing aircraft programs and emerged from the Joint Advanced Strike Technology (JAST) program, as a result of the Clinton Administration's bottom-up review of US defence policy. It had, thus, both economic and war-fighting objectives. The US fighter fleet was aging and perceived as becoming obsolete relative for future needs. Competition for the contract started in 1996 with three firms: Lockheed Martin, the McDonnel

Douglas/British Aerospace/Northrop Grumman team, and Boeing. For the concept demonstration phase, Lockheed Martin and Boeing were selected. As for the engine, Congress decided to pursue an alternative program to be developed by GE Transportation Aircraft Engine by Rolls-Royce, in addition to the F135 primary engine produced by Pratt & Whitney in order to stimulate competition, envisioning cost savings. This program ended near renewed Milestone B baseline set in 2012, and General Electric/Rolls-Royce became a subcontractor of Pratt & Whitney, assuming responsibility for developing the vertical lift system for the F-35B.

The F-35 was innovative and posed many technological challenges. The F-35s are fighter jets, which combine composite materials, stealth technology, advanced radar and sensor, and thrust vectoring and integrated avionics, generating situational awareness. Strike fighters are dual-role tactical fighters which are capable of both air-to-ground and air-to-air combat. The system operates as a network, detecting further information needs, prioritizing them, and issuing new commands to the sensors considered most appropriate to satisfy these needs. Identification and tracking continue automatically in a closed-loop fashion as new data from on-board or off-board sensors is acquired. These, in turn, can be either relayed to other platforms in 'open transmit' mode or, subject to data bring-back memory capability, manually recorded and stored. The results of the fusion process are provided to the pilot/vehicle interface for display, fire control for weapon support, and electronic warfare for countermeasures support.[12] The main feature of the F-35 architecture was to be the interactivity among the different combat systems, so that the functional outcomes and capabilities were to be generated synergistically.

The data from on-board sensors and off-board sources would be integrated to the F-35's central computer, therefore providing a precise view of the tactical situation. To this is added stealth capability, already discussed in the previous section. The goal of the program was to achieve an acceptable level of stealth while securing manoeuvrability without exceeding production costs. The aircraft is built using glass fibre honeycomb loaded with carbon, working along its less disciplined shape, to provide very low RCS. Furthermore, the F-35 features a low observable substance called fibre mat, carbon nanotube-infused fibres that can absorb or reflect radar. This is built into the composite 'skin' of the aircraft. The program also included a HMDS (Helmet Mounted Display System), which along with other technical issues represents a great technological challenge and generates debate and criticism regarding delays and costs among auditing agencies and key actors. A design with commonalities for the three services

---

[12] For a detailed assessment, see Petrelli, 2020.

was aimed at avoiding duplicated costs, but diverse service requirements into a common design would be a major factor for F-35s technological challenges and, thus, outcomes.

An interesting feature of the F-35, especially concerning defence economics, is concept of international effort. During its development, ten international partners joined development and production efforts, or as buyers: Australia, Canada, Denmark, Italy, Israel, Japan, the Netherlands, Norway, South Korea, Turkey, and the UK. This entails several issues such as technology transfers, impacts on national industries, commitment to alliances, and so forth. The idea was to benefit from economies of scale, avoid duplicating R&D efforts within the alliance, and strengthen overall deterrence capacity of the partners, which would have access to cutting-edge technology. During development, however, critical issues have been subject to dispute within the international collaboration effort, such as the United States' purpose of retaining the core technological features. Problems regarding technology transfer, especially in the case of a defection from the alliance, as would be the case with Turkey, have also been a matter for scrutiny. The procurement was to be within the United States. Therefore, United States' domestic issues and BP politics have also affected other countries.

Despite its periodic progress the history of F-35 has been marked by repeated cost overruns, delays, and other setbacks which have 'made it appear that its competition and successful deployment will never be achieved' (Chapman, 2019, p. 89). From the very beginning, the F-35 seemed to signal a possible tense procurement story and ultimate failure. However, I claim here that evolution of threat level, with the return to a scenario of great power competition, congressional support – despite scrutiny and debate – and the program's eventual evolution and successful feasibility demonstrations, places the project on the successful spectrum. Different from the B-2 and the FCS, decision-makers supported the program since the need for the F-35 was clear. Three forces pressuring decision-makers also contributed to the program's deployment and maturing, since together they held more power in the budgetary arena. The program reached Milestone B in 2001, the year the Lockheed was awarded the System Design and Development Contract along with the partnered-up Northrop Grumman and BAE. From 2001 to 2012, while in System Development and Demonstration, tests and Low-Rate Initial Production, the program encountered several difficulties in meeting its projections, especially due to cost overruns.

Unlike the B-2, Congress and other actors have remained mostly supportive of the program. Even though they were also demanding further scrutinization and optimization of costs, the debate centred more around how to make it work rather than cancelling. From 2001 to 2012, however, the F-35 faced serious issues, breaching the Nunn-McCurdy amendment[13] in 2010, and being the target of constant scrutiny and criticism. The GAO reports on cost and schedule overruns were constant. Up to the re-approval of the program into Milestone B and the new Acquisition Program Baseline of 2012, the progress of the JSF within the acquisition spectrum was slow. There was criticism and debate over the program's funding, cost growth, and performance issues.

It is argued here that the evolution of threat level, the widespread constituency interests involved in the program, the downsizing of competition for resources among forces since it is a multi-force program, and the lack of an alternative program that could satisfy the need for the fighter created a higher level of consensus among political actors.

The workforce and subcontractors are spread around the United States with facilities in geographic locations potentially represented by 90 US Senators and 424 US representatives. Differently from the FCS, although highly innovative and still in development, the F-35 has demonstrated increasing technological feasibility and performance over the years, while the FCS never reached operational capability. Furthermore, as the years passed and threat level rose, the three forces have been able to create a narrative for the need of the F-35 that convinced Congress.

Chapman (2019) investigates the possible scenarios in which the F-35 might be deployed for engaging threats. The F-35 is suitable for engaging in possible threats coming from terrorism, China, North Korea, Iran, and Russia. The assurance of the ability to credibly back up the Asia-Pacific pivot was especially necessary. The F-35 could be used in an air-to-sea concept of battle in the region. Furthermore, deterrence of Russia's pivot to the East is a major challenge. The author evaluates that despite the program's problems, 'the United States will ultimately be more concerned with the geopolitical consequences of potentially losing air superiority to probable enemies than with the protracted problems JSF has experienced over the past two decades' (Chapman, 2019, p. 115). Threat level, especially emerging from China and Russia, 'will sustain the JSF even with doubts over its technical capabilities, whether its operational range is sufficient for

---

[13] In 1981, Senator Sam Nunn and Representative David McCurdy introduced what became known as the NunnMcCurdy amendment to the 1982 defence spending legislation. The Nunn-McCurdy legislation established congressional oversight of defense acquisition systems whose procurement acquisition unit cost (PAUC) and average procurement unit cost (APUC) costs growth exceeds 15 per cent. In this case, the Secretary of Defense has an obligation to tell Congress. If cost growth surpasses 25 per cent, the Secretary must provide Congress with a written declaration providing the legislators with the reasons of the breach. Otherwise, the program would be canceled.

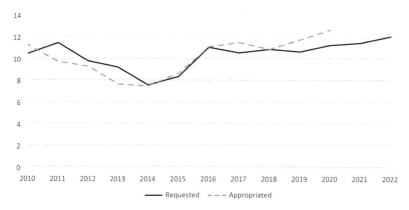

Figure 6 Requested versus appropriated amount for the F-35 (current dollars)
Source: Comptroller, DoD, 2023. The Author.

combat missions, mechanical problems, or costs (Chapman, 2019, p. 347)'. A growing threat impacts directly the decision to mobilize resources and thus is positively related to the success of large-scale projects. Figure 7 shows that despite cost and schedule delays, stakeholder needs, perform-ance, and growing threat levels stabilized procurement in the F-35. There were no viable and better options for stakeholders. Figure 7 clearly demon-strates that despite delays and cost overruns, Congress remained faithful to the program since effectiveness, and, more importantly, stakeholders' needs are more important than efficiency in defence markets.

Figure 7 shows a relatively high level of consensus among the Executive and the Congress on the F-35. This is briefly explained next. On 28 February 2012, Senator Kelly Ayotte briefed Pacific Command Commander Admiral Robert F. Willard about the importance of the F-35 for the Asia-Pacific region. Admiral Willard answered that in the light of Chinese aircraft development there was no suitable alternatives to the F-35. The Chief of Naval Operations subscribed to Willard's argument, highlighting the importance of F-35's stealth capacity. Answering to a congressional hearing, Marine Corps Assistant Commandant John M. Paxton stated that the F-35B STOVL triples the number of global airfields that can be used, and combined with the F-35 C doubles the number of US capital ships capable of operating the fighter. Paxton highlighted the import-ance of the fighter in order to counter the threats of state and non-state actors and A2/AD technology,[14] stressing that to reach such targets, the United States would have to successfully develop the F-35 (Chapman, 2019). On April 2016,

---

[14] Anti-access and area denial (A2/AD) is a military strategy aimed at preventing an adversary from entering or operating within a specific area.

Senator Orrin Hatch spoke in support of the JSF on the floor, emphasizing that despite the frustrations with the acquisition system regarding costs and schedule, the emergence of geopolitical threats such as Russia's annexation of Crimea, China's growing assertiveness, and North Korean and Iranian advancing nuclear capabilities, the F-35 was needed to penetrate advanced enemy air defences and to strike ground targets. Senator Orrin also argued that unit costs were dropping as procurement progressed (Chapman, 2019). General support in Congress continues. On 5 May 2021, twenty senators from both parties signed a letter urging funding for modernization and sustainment costs of the JSF, in the light of Russia's and China's advances in their air defence systems and their own fifth-generation fighters. This letter followed a similar one from the House, in which 132 representatives also demonstrated support for the program (Stone, 2021). The need for the F-35 in face of the growing external threat and the lack of suitable options for the fighter are strong justifications for congressional funding despite schedule and cost overruns. Three forces advocating for the program certainly give it more stability in the bureaucratic arena.

In the period after 2012, cost and schedule overruns were attenuated when compared to initial projections of the program. The program development stabilized and moved forward roughly as planned. 'The program achieved significant successes during this period, including a rapidly declining production cost, and initial operating capacity for the USAF, USMC, and the Israeli Air Force'. Chapman (2019, p. 357) evaluated that 'technological obsolescence of combat aircraft against military enemies is even more dangerous than an expensive and long-delayed military system'. The program, however, cannot be considered as a full success on the spectrum. In its 2017 report on the JSF, the GAO found that there were still many problems with the program, including spare parts shortages, undefined technical data needs, and unfunded intermediate-level maintenance capabilities (GAO, 2017). The GAO also estimated that the United States had spent almost $400 billion on the program, making it the DoD's most expensive program in history, with additional projected $276 billion in procurement and estimating that the overall fleet operational and costs associated with the aircraft's lifetime would exceed 1$ trillion. The program was billions of dollars overbudget and seven years behind schedule. While entering the IOT&E (Initial Operational Test and Evaluation) in 2018 and aiming at soon entering Milestone C (Full-Production Decision), the JSF still had many unresolved deficiencies, thirteen of them classified by Director of Operational Test and Evaluation (DOT&E) as 'must fix' (CRS, 2020). The program was billions of dollars overbudget and seven years behind schedule.

On the one hand, cost and schedule overruns are important criteria for evaluating the success or failure of large-scale defence projects. Moreover, during the project's lifecycle, cost and schedule are indicators of possible problems with technological feasibility and different projects are in competition for resources with one another. This can affect stakeholder's and decision-makers' support for the project, making it more prone to fail. On the other hand, as demonstrated, the necessity of the project to major stakeholders, its operational success, and hence what the innovation provides to national defence have more weight in defining a successful project. This places the F-35 on the successful spectrum of large-scale defence projects. Regarding efficiency criteria, despite the project initially demonstrating poor results, it ultimately reached production with better cost and schedule results. Furthermore, the F-35 proved its necessity and operational performance.

The F-35 is currently in low-rate initial production, with 894 aircraft delivered as of the beginning of 2023. The program is expected to reach Milestone C and Full Rate Production Decision Review by the end of 2023. Authors tend to agree that JSF has suffered many problems due to expenditure and delays. Nonetheless, due to external threat and national defence necessities, they consider that the program is needed. According to Chapman (2019), 'combat effectiveness and performance of the JSF is the bottom line indicator of whether the expenditure and delays have been worthwhile'. Although the F-35 has not engaged in major combat operations, it was used against Iranian and Hezbollah targets near Beirut and received positive assessment from stakeholders like the IAF (Israeli Air Force). Deptula (2020) states that the Armed Forces need the fifth-generation fighter as the requirements dictated by the global threat environment demand nothing less. He argues that the F-35 operational performance is 'an easy piece of homework to grade' (Deptula, 2020, p. 1). The author highlights that the F-35 is the only fifth-generation fighter in production in the Western world. 'If you want the attributes of stealth, electronic warfare, sensors, processing power, and real-time teaming all fused into one fighter package, this aircraft is it. F-35s have already gone to war and the results speak for themselves' (Deptula, 2020, p. 1). John Venable (2020) states that the F-35 is now the world's most dominant multi-role fighter and provides a significant competitive advantage over peer competitors. Venable holds that the 'F-35A's capabilities and decreasing price tag make it both vital to the nation's defence and more cost-effective than fourth-generation fighters' (Venable, 2020, p. 1).

Hlatky and Rice (2018, p. 34) state that, given its capabilities, 'it is becoming increasingly obvious that there is no alternative to the F-35 program'. The Pentagon has declared that, despite cost overruns and delays, the F-35 is still a top priority. Chapman (2019, p. 347) argues that 'JSF critics need to present economically and militarily credible alternatives to address emerging US and allied jet fighter combat operational needs against emerging threats beyond maintaining existing combat aircraft fleets'. According to Chapman (2019), threat level, especially those emerging from China and Russia, made the JSF necessary, and that 'will also sustain the JSF even with doubts over its technical capabilities, whether its operational range is sufficient for combat missions, mechanical problems, and cost' (2019, p. 137).

According to Chapman, developing and advancing military jet fighter technology is a never-ending process. Countries such as Russia and China are willing to make financial investments to develop their own fighters based on advancing their national interests. This threatens the United States and its allies since these countries continue to perfect their own fifth-generation fighters 'leaving the United States to not assume air superiority as a given' (Abplanalp, 2017, p. 26). In other words, there is a clear need for large-scale projects such as F-35.

Authors agree that there is a need to develop a jet fighter program capable of meeting the military requirements for the second decade of the twenty-first century. Countries like North Korea, Iran, Russia, and China along with terrorism threaten the United States, and the F-35 is pivotal in US strategic assessment of possible future combat engagement and to avoid losing air superiority (Chapman, 2019). The United States and its allies want to ensure 'their ability to credibly back up the Asia-Pacific Pivot, European Deterrence Initiative, and deter Russia's pivot to the East' (Chapman, 2019, p. 357).

The most problematic issue is the total life cost of maintaining the fleet, which has been estimated to surpasses $1 trillion (Chapman, 2019). The debate centres around efficiency versus effectiveness. Despite efficiency issues of cost and delays, major stakeholders view the F-35 as necessary to national security, and its performance has been proven effective to fulfil its initial conception purposes.

Up until the present moment, the results of the F-35 are close to its initial conception, purposes, and objectives. Initial cost and schedule overruns were attenuated, although in this regard the F-35 did not keep up, and is not keeping up, with its initial estimates. This is a result of resource mobilization and innovation being positively related to the rise of external threat.

The elasticity of demand was lower than the case of the B-2. In the absence of substitutes, demand tends towards inelastic. This indicates a middle-rage technological feasibility status for the F-35. Challenges have been put forward by GAO and other analyses, but advancements constantly recognized. Technological feasibility proved itself through tests and operations during Milestone B, which therefore did not weaken the project as much as the cases of the FCS and the B-2.

Table 3 F-35 projections and results

Initial objectives	Results
Cost projection: $177 billion (2001 dollars)	1.7 trillion (2023 dollars)
Quantity projection:	1,000 units
Schedule: IOC by 2011	Achieved: IOC by 2015
Performance: Multi-role jet fighter to ensure air superiority	Achieved
Operational success:	Achieved
Stakeholder's need: Deterrence against China, Russia and other enemies	Achieved

Source: The Author. US Comptroller Office.

The project has not been greatly modified, in technological terms, throughout its development regarding its initial goals. This places the future tendency of the JSF on the successful spectrum of high-scale defence projects, as conceptualized by this Element. As Table 3 demonstrates, all effectiveness criteria have been met. There was a small delay in initial operational capability, but the fighter already delivered more than 1,000 units. Cost projections were readjusted by the year of 2012, as already argued, and they certainly are large. All criteria considered, however, the objective of air superiority was accomplished by the F-35. It is not entirely successful because of cost, but it is considered in the successful spectrum.

Congress is more concerned with deficit levels and fiscal austerity. It must attend to several interests and disputes for resources. Nonetheless, as argued, Congress has been firmly backed with high consensus among parochial interests regarding the F-35, related to job creation and campaign support. However, this Element argues that this is not enough. The program has to prove itself worth the possible efficiency flaws experienced, in the case of the F-35, in its costs and schedule delays. The F-35 has gathered consensus in Congress and the Executive because of its need, promising operational value and the lack of cost-effective options. The three forces acting together to protect the program certainly gives it more bureaucratic power, and, thus, the ability to obtain resources and develop the project. Differently from the B-2, Congress and other key decision-makers are more concerned with making it work than searching for available options. This is reflected in the amount requested by the Executive and the amount appropriated by Congress, demonstrating a consensus between the two branches of government. The tendency is continuous support for the program, since the variables applied here remain.

As the variables predicted, growing threat level, *stakeholder* need, and proved technological feasibility, besides the downsizing of marginal costs, have resulted in the F-35 enduring, while the other programs did not. Even though it is the most expensive defence program in history, it does not lack the *necessary conditions* for success that the FCS and the B-2 did.

4 Concluding Remarks

In this Element, I analysed the political economy of large-scale defence projects. More specifically, I attempted to build a model to explain the success or failure of innovative large-scale projects. In order to do so, after establishing efficiency and effectiveness success criteria, I constructed hypotheses from three different angles of analysis: the International System, the economic and technological basis of innovation, and the domestic political arena. Each of these angles was translated into an independent variable, namely: level of threat, technological feasibility, and level of consensus. I argued that technological feasibility and political consensus are necessary and conjointly sufficient conditions to explain the success or failure of large-scale defence projects, while external threat has a positive and strong correlation with the level of success of these projects. This model was first presented in a causal linear form. However, the relation among the variables was further explored and a systemic approach was delineated. This hypothesis was then corroborated by scrutinizing three cases: FCS, B-2, and F-35, assessing independently each variable and its relation to the dependent variable. The model generated results which may be summarized as in Tables 4 and 5.

Defence markets are not regular markets. In the demand side, they are monopsonistic domestically and can be competitive internationally. In the supply side, they can be oligopolistic or monopolistic. Imperfect information, large control by the government, high costs of capital, and human factors among other things make entry barriers high. Exit barriers are also high since

Table 4 The success or failure of large-scale defence projects

	External threat	Political consensus	Technological feasibility	Success or failure
B–2	High to low	Medium to low	Low to high	Failed spectrum
FCS	Low	Medium to low	Low	Unsuccessful
F–35	Low to high	Medium to high	Medium to high	Successful spectrum

Source: The Author.

Table 5 SC and the projects analysed

	Cost overruns	Schedule overruns	Performance	Stakeholder's need	Operational success	Success or failure
B–2	High	Medium	Medium	Low	Medium	Failed spectrum
FCS	High	High	Low	Low	Low	Unsuccessful
F–35	Medium	High	High	High	Medium	Successful spectrum

Source: The Author.

conversion to civil products is difficult. The projects analysed here are projects that the firms could afford to lose or win (to bet), although not with major setbacks in the case of procurement cuts. Politicians play a decisive role, even though theoretically the Armed Forces have a better technical and threat analysis know-how. But they are bureaucracies. They will maximize their budget, prestige, and area of actuation. This will create a complex domestic scenario. To summarize, defence markets are full of imperfections.

Tables 4 and 5 demonstrate that stakeholders' needs can sustain a project throughout its development, even though there are cost and schedule overruns. The F-35 was needed, differently from the B-2 in the early 1990s and the FCS. The ultimate decision is political. It can be argued that economics also drives politics. This is true. Clinton's bottom-up review is a clear example. But in times of threat and considering the characteristics of the industry, the tendency is rising budgets and large-scale projects. The B-2, as summarized in Table 4, achieved production and was commissioned in several conventional missions. However, despite not being considered a complete failure, it is in the failed spectrum. The initial plans, the delays and cost overruns, stakeholders' opposition to its procurement, and its possibilities of substitution did not make it a success.

The study of large-scale defence projects and how innovation works in the defence sector is a fruitful ground for research with many possibilities for enquiry. The model presented here was intended to provide a useful framework for analysis, but it can still be further developed. The variables and parameters proposed would benefit from the use of quantitative techniques, for example. The study would also gain from the expansion and generalization of the model, with the necessary adjustments, to other countries and projects. The model does not necessarily be limited to analyse innovative-capable countries or well-developed democracies in which there is 'pulling and hauling'. Proper adaptations can be made, and the ideas put forward here can be applied to other projects and countries.

References

Abplanalp, Jetta. (2017). *Air Superiority: Is the F-35 Aircraft Worth the Cost?* Maxwell Air Force Base, AL: United States Air Command and Staff College Air University.

Adams, Gordon and Williams, Cindy. (2010). *Buying National Security: How America Plans and Pays for Its Global Role and Safety at Home*. New York: Routledge.

Allison, Graham. (1969). *Essence of Decision: Explaining the Cuban Missile Crisis*. Boston, MA: Little, Brown.

Allison, Graham T. and Halperin, Morton H. (1972). Bureaucratic Politics: A Paradigm and Some Policy Implications. *World Politics*, v. 24, n. 1, pp. 48–80.

Amarante, José C.A. (2012). Texto Para discussão 1758: A Base Industrial de Defesa. IPEA.

Andrade, Israel de Oliveira. (2016). *A Base Industrial De Defesa: Contextualização Histórica, Conjuntura Atual E Perspectivas Futuras*. Rio de Janeiro: IPEA.

Brockman, Heide. (2017). *US Defense Budget Outcomes: Volatility and Predictability in Army Weapons Funding*. West Point, NY: United States Military Academy & Palgrave Macmillan.

Brower, Michael. (1990). B-2 New Numbers, Old Arguments. *Bulletin of the Atomic Scientists*, v. 46, n. 5, pp. 25–29.

Brown, Michael E. (1988). *B-2 or Not B-2 Crisis and Choice in the US Strategic Bomber Program*. Survival: Global Politics and Strategy, v. 30, n. 4, pp. 351–366.

Candreva, Philip J. (2017). *National Defense Budgeting and Financial Management: Policy and Practice*. Charlotte, NC: Information Age Publishing, Inc.

CBO. (1993). *CBO Staff Memorandum: Alternative Procurement Programs for the B-2 bomber: Effects on Capability and Costs*. Washington, DC: The Congress of the United States Congressional Budget Office.

Chapman, Bert. (2019). *Global Defense Procurement and the F-35 Joint Strike Fighter*. Cham: Palgrave Macmillan, e-book.

Clausewitz, Carl Von. (2007). *On War*. Oxford: Oxford University Press.

CRS. (2020). F-35 Joint Strike Fighter (JSF) Program. Washington DC: Congressional Research Service.

Dall'agnol, Gustavo Fornari. (2022). *Defense, Decision-Making and Political Economy: Large-Scale Projects and the Decision-Making Process in United*

States' Defense Politics. Belo Horizonte: PUC-MG. www.biblioteca.pucminas
.br/teses/RelacoesInternacionais_GustavoFornariDallagnol_29820_
Textocompleto.pdf.

Dall'Agnol, G. F. and Dall'Agnol, Augusto César. (2020). NATO's Decision-
Making Process in Budgeting: Prospects of the Burden-Sharing Problem.
Revista Política Hoje, v. 29, n. 2. https://periodicos.ufpe.br/revistas/politica
hoje/article/download/248717/38812.

Demarest, Heidi Brockman. (2017). *US Defense Budget Outcomes: Volatility
and Predictability in Army Weapons Funding.* Cham: Palgrave Macmillan.

Deptula, Dave. (2020). *F-35 Is Performing Far Better than Critics Would Have
You Think.* www.forbes.com/sites/davedeptula/2020/07/20/f-35-problem-
child-or-on-track-forsuccess/?sh=5fe6082e15d1. Accessed at: December,
2021.

Diamond, David. (2006). Defence Innovation: Internal and External Factors.
RUSI Defence Systems.

Dunne, J. Paul. (1995). The Defense Industrial Base. In Sandler, T. and Hartley, K.
(eds.). *Handbook of Defense Economics* . North Holand: Elselvier Science B.V,
pp. 400–430.

Edquist, Charles. (ed.). (1997). *Systems of Innovation.* London: Pinter.

Elias, Norbert. (1993). *O Processo Civilizador: Formação do Estado e Civilização.*
Rio de Janeiro: Zahar.

Ellman, Jesse E. (2009). *The Role of Evolutionary Acquisition and Spiral
Development in the Failure of the Army's Future Combat System.* Washington,
DC: Georgetown University.

Elman, Colin. (1999). *The Logic of Emulation: The Diffusion of Military
Practices in the International System.* Columbia: Columbia University.

Fagerberg, Jan and Godinho, Manuel M. 2006. Innovation and Catching-Up. In
Fagerberg, J., Mowery, D. and Richard N. (eds.). *The Oxford Handbook of
Innovation.* Oxford: Oxford University Press, pp. 514–598.

Freedman, Lawrence. (1976). Logic, Politics and Foreign Policy Processes:
A Critique of the Bureaucratic Politics Model. *International Affairs (Royal
Institute of International Affairs).* v. 52, n. 3, pp. 434–449.

Freeman, Christopher. (1987). *Technology, Policy, and Economic Performance:
Lessons from Japan.* New York: Pinter.

GAO. (1990). *Report to the Chairman, Committee on Armed Services, House of
Representatives. Strategic Bombers: B-2 Program Status and Current Issues.*
Washington, DC: United States General Accounting Office.

GAO. (1995). *B-2 Bomber: Status of Cost, Development and Production.*
Washington, DC: United States General Accounting Office.

GAO. (2005). *Assessments of Selected Major Weapon Programs*. Washington, DC: Government Accountability Office.

GAO. (2017). F-35 Aircraft Sustainment: DOD Needs to Address Challenges Affecting Readiness and Cost Transparency. Washington, DC: Government Accountability Office.

Gouré, Daniel. (2021). *Future Combat System: What Went Wrong?* www .lexingtoninstitute.org/future-combat-system-what-went-wrong/. Accessed at: November, 2021.

Gourevitch, Peter. (1978). The Second Image Reversed: The International Sources of Domestic Politics. *International Organization*, v. 32, n. 4, pp. 881–911.

Grant, Rebecca. (2012). Black Bomb: The B-2's Tortured Acquisition Program. *Air Force Magazine*, January. www.airforcemag.com/PDF/MagazineArchive/ Documents/2012/January%202012/0112bomber.pdf. Accessed at: October, 2022.

Halperin, Morton H. (1974). *Bureaucratic Politics and Foreign Policy*. Washington, DC: Brookings Institution.

Hartley, Keith. (1995). Industrial Policies in the Defense Sector. In Sandler, T. and Hartley, K. (eds.). *Handbook of Defense Economics*. North Holand: Elselvier Science B.V, pp. 460–489.

Hartley, Keith. (2020). *Defence Economics*. Cambridge: Cambridge University Press.

Hartley, Keith and Sandler, Todd. (eds.). (1990). *The Economics of Defence Spending: An International Survey*. London: Routledge.

Healy, Melissa. (1990). Cost of $1.95 billion for Each B-2 Held Possible: Defense: The Price Would Soar if Fewer Are Built and Procurement Is Extended, a Congressional Report Says. Cancellation Would Save $45 billion. *The LA Times*, April, 1990. www.latimes.com/archives/la-xpm-1990-04-04-mn-711-story.html. Accessed at: October, 2012.

Herz, John H. (1950). Idealist Internationalism and the Security Dilemma. *World Politics*, v. 2, n. 2, pp. 157–180.

Hlatky, Stéfanie and Rice, Jeffrey. (2018). Striking a Deal on the F-35: Multinational Politics and US Defence Acquisition. *Defence Studies*, v. 18, n. 1, pp. 1–21.

Kaeser, Hans Ulrich. (2009). *The Future Combat System: What Future Can the Army Afford?* Washington, DC: Center for Strategic & International Studies.

Krasner, Stephen D. (1972). Are Bureaucracies Important? (Or Allison's Wonderland)? *Foreign Policy*, v.1, n. 7, pp. 159–179.

Laffont, J.-J, and Tirole, J. (1986). Using Cost Observation to Regulate Firms. *Journal of Political Economy*. v. 94, n. 3, pp. 614–641.

Lijphart, Arend. (1971). Comparative Politics and the Comparative Method. *The American Political Science Review*, v. 65, n. 3, pp. 534–546.

Mearsheimer, John J. (2014). *The Tragedy of Great Power Politics*. New York: W.W Norton.

Moore, Molly. (1989). B2 Bomber Cancellation Is Urged. *The Washington Post*, 19 May. www.google.com/search?q=B2+BOMBER+CANCELLATION+IS +URGED.+The+Washington+Post%3A+May+19%2C+1989.&rlz= 1C1CHBD_pt-PTBR924BR924&oq=B2+BOMBER+CANCELLATION+IS +URGED.+The+Washington+Post%3A+May+19%2C+1989.&aqs=chrome ..69i57.784j0j4&sourceid=chrome&ie=UTF-8. Accessed at: October, 2022.

Mowery, David G. (2010). Military R&D and Innovation. In Hall, B. H. and Rosenberg, N. (eds.). *Handbook of the Economics of Innovation*. Columbia: Elsevier. Vol. 2, pp. 1219–1256.

Neustadt, Richard E. (2008). Poder Presidencial E Os Presidentes Modernos: A Política De Liderança De Roosevelt a Reagan. Brasília: Enap.

Olson, Mancur and Zeckhauser, Richard. (1996). An Economic Theory of Alliances. *Review of Economics and Statistics*. v. 48, n. 3, pp. 266–279.

Palmer, Glenn, McManus, Roseanne W., D'Orazio, Vito et al. (2020). The MID5 Dataset, 2011–2014: Procedures, Coding Rules, and Description. *Conflict Management and Peace Science*, v. 39, n. 4, pp. 470–482. https:// journals.sagepub.com/doi/full/10.1177/0738894221995743.

Peck, M. J., and Scherer, F. M. 1962. *The Weapons Acquisition Process: An Economic Analysis*. Cambridge, MA: Harvard University Press.

Pernin, Christopher G., Axelband, Elliot, and Wilson, Peter A. (2012). *Lessons from the Army's Future Combat Systems Program*. Santa Monica, CA: RAND Corporation.

Petrelli, Niccolò. (2020). *Lessons from the F-35 Programme*. Roma: Instituto Affari Internazionali.

Posen, Barry. (1984). *The Sources of Military Doctrine: France, Britain, and Germany between the World Wars*. Ithaca, NY: Cornell University Press.

Ranga, Marina and Etzkowitz, Henry. (2013). Triple Helix Systems: An Analytical Framework for Innovation Policy and Practice in the Knowledge Society. *Industry & Higher Education*, v. 27, n. 3, pp. 237–262.

Resende-Santos. (2007). *Neorealism, States, and Modern Mass Army*. Cambridge: Cambridge University Press.

Rogerson, William P. (1995). Incentive Models of the Defense Procurement Process. In Sandler, T. and Hartley, K. (eds.). *Handbook of Defense Economics*. North Holand: Elselvier Science B.V, pp. 310–347.

Schilling, Warner R. (1961). The H-Bomb Decision: How to Decide without Actually Choosing. *Political Science Quarterly*, v. 76, n. 1, pp. 73–90.

Rosati, Jarel . (1981). Developing a Systematic Decision-Making Framework: Bureaucratic Politics in Perspective. *World Politics*, v. 33, n. 2, pp. 234–252.

Rosen, S. (1991). *Winning the Next War: Innovation and the Modern Military.* Ithaca: Cornell University Press.

Sabatier, Paul, A., and Jenkins-Smith, Hank. (1993). *Policy Change and Learning: An Advocacy Coalition Approach.* Boulder, CO: Westview Press.

Sabatier, P. A, and Jenkins-Smith, H. (2007). The Advocacy Coalition Framework: An Assessment. In Sabatier, P. (ed.). *Theories of the Policy Process.* Boulder, CO: Westview Press, pp. 117–166.

Sabatier, Paul A. and Weible, Christopher M. (2007). The Advocacy Coalition Framework: Innovations and Clarifications. In Sabatier, Paul A. (org.). *Theories of Policy Process.* Boulder: West View Press, p. 350.

Schofield, S. (1993). Defence Technology, Industrial Structure and Arms Conversion. In Coopey, R., Uttley, M. and Sporadi, G. (eds.). *Defence Science and Technology: Adjusting to Change.* Harwood: Reading.

Schumpeter, Joseph. (1934). *The Theory of Economic Development.* Cambridge, MA: Harvard University Press.

Schumpeter, J. (1966). *Invention and Economic Growth.* Cambridge, MA: Harvard University Press.

Simon, Herbert A. (1965). *Administrative Behavior: A Study of Decision-Making Processes in Administrative Organization.* New York: Free Press.

Singer, J. David. (1987). Reconstructing the Correlates of War Dataset on Material Capabilities of States, 1816–1985. *International Interactions*, v. 14, pp. 115–132.

SIPRI. (2020). *SIPRI Yearbook.* Oxford: Blackwell, Oxford (for Stockholm International Peace Research Institute).

Sprenger, Sebastian. (2016). 30 Years: Future Combat Systems: Acquisition Gone Wrong. *Defense News*, October, 2016. www.defensenews.com/30th-annivesary/2016/10/25/30-years-future-combatsystems-acquisition-gone-wrong/. Accessed at: November, 2022.

Stacy, Jerry and Gunzinger, Mark. (1996). *Bureaucratic Politics and the B-2 Bomber: The FY'96 Budget as a Case Study.* Washington, DC: Naval War College.

Stone, Mike. (2022). *Bipartisan U.S. senators pen support for funding of F-35 jet.* www.reuters.com/world/us/bipartisan-us-senators-pen-support-funding-f-35-jet-2021-05-06/. Accessed at: December, 2022.

Tilly, Charles. (1990). Coercion, Capital, and European States AD 990-1990. Cambridge, Massachusetts: Basil Blackwell, Inc.

True, James L., Jones, Bryan D. and Baumgartner, Frank. (2007). Punctuated-Equilibrium Theory: Explaining Stability and Change in Public Policymaking. In Sabatier, Paul A. (org). *Theories of the Policy Process*. Boulder: West View Press, pp. 155–189.

Tsebelis, George. (2005). Veto Players and Institutional Analysis. *Governance: An International Journal of Policy and Administration*, v. 13, n. 4, pp. 441–474.

Undersecretary of Defense (Comptroller). (2020). DoD Budget Request: Washington DC: https://comptroller.defense.gov/Budget-Materials/. Accessed at: December, 2022.

Venable, John. (2020). *The F-35A Is the World's Most Dominant, Cost-Effective Fighter: The Air Force Needs to Accelerate Its Acquisition Now*. Washington, DC: The Heritage Foundation (Center for National Defense).

Walker, W., Graham, M. and Harbor, B. (1988). From Components to Integrated Systems: Technological Diversity and Interactions between Military and Civilian Sectors. In Gummett, P. and Reppy, J. (eds.). *The Relation between Military and Civilian Technologies*. Dordrecht: Kluwer Academic, pp. 17–37.

Walt, Sephen M. (1987). *The Origins of Alliances*. New York: Cornell University Press.

Waltz, Kenneth. (1979). *Theory of International Politics*. Reading, MA: Addison-Wesley.

Waltz, Kenneth. (1996). International Politics Is Not Foreign Policy. *Security Studies*, v. 6, n. 1, pp. 54–57.

Watts, Barry. (2008). *The US Defense Industrial Base: Past, Present and Future*. Washington, DC: CSBA.

Welch, Jasper. (1989). Assessing the Value of Stealthy Aircraft and Cruise Missiles. *International Security*, v. 14, n. 2, pp. 47–63.

Welch, David A. (1998). A Positive Science of Bureaucratic Politics? *Mershon International Studies Review*, v. 42, n. 2, pp. 210–216.

Wildavsky, Aaron. (1964). *The Politics of the Budgetary Process*. Boston: Little, Brown.

Acknowledgements

I am grateful to Professor Eugenio Pacelli Lazzarotti Diniz Costa, Rashmi Singh, David R. Mares, and Keith Hartley for helpful comments and suggestions. Needless to say, the responsibility for the final form of the Element rests entirely with me.

About the Author

Gustavo Fornari Dall'Agnol holds a PhD in International Politics and works as a consultant, teacher (having taught at PUC-MG and UFSC), and researcher focusing on decision-making with special emphasis on international and governmental politics, defence industry and innovation. He is working with a grant issued by CAPES/INCT on the project INCT: 'Observatório de Capacidades Militares e Políticas de Defesa'. He is Senior Fellow at the South American Institute of Politics and Strategy (ISAPE), an independent think tank based in Brazil.

Cambridge Elements $\equiv$

Defence Economics

Keith Hartley

University of York

Keith Hartley was Professor of Economics and Director of the Centre for Defence Economics at the University of York, where he is now Emeritus Professor of Economics. He is the author of over 500 publications comprising journal articles, books and reports. His most recent books include *The Economics of Arms* (Agenda Publishing, 2017) and with Jean Belin (Eds) *The Economics of the Global Defence Industry* (Taylor and Francis, 2020). Hartley was founding Editor of the journal *Defence and Peace Economics*; a NATO Research Fellow; a QinetiQ Visiting Fellow; consultant to the UN, EC, EDA, UK MoD, HM Treasury, Trade and Industry, Business, Innovation and Skills and International Development and previously Special Adviser to the House of Commons Defence Committee.

About the Series

Defence Economics is a relatively new field within the discipline of economics. It studies all aspects of the economics of war and peace. It embraces a wide range of topics in both macroeconomics and microeconomics. Cambridge Elements in Defence Economics aims to publish original and authoritative papers in the field. These will include expert surveys of the foundations of the discipline, its historical development and contributions developing new and novel topics. They will be valuable contributions to both research and teaching in universities and colleges, and will also appeal to other specialist groups comprising politicians, military and industrial personnel as well as informed general readers.

Cambridge Elements $\equiv$

Defence Economics

Elements in the Series

Printed in the United States
by Baker & Taylor Publisher Services